STAGFLATION

AN INTERNATIONAL
PROBLEM

BUSINESS ECONOMICS AND FINANCE

a series of monographs and textbooks

Executive Editor

Arthur B. Laffer

Department of Economics
University of Chicago
Graduate School of Business
Chicago, Illinois

Other Volumes in Preparation.

STAGFLATION

AN INTERNATIONAL PROBLEM

Edited by RANDALL HINSHAW

MARCEL DEKKER INC.   New York and Basel

Library of Congress Cataloging in Publication Data
Main entry under title:

Stagflation.

(Business economics and finance ; v. 10)
Contributions to the 5th Bologna-Claremont
conference, held at Scripps College, Claremont,
Calif., in 1975, which discussed International
aspects of the world economic crisis.
Includes indexes.
1. Inflation (Finance) and unemployment--
Congresses. I. Hinshaw, Randall Weston.
HG3881.S69   332.4'1   77-21824
ISBN 0-8247-6644-X

Marcel Dekker, Inc.
270 Madison Avenue, New York, New York 10016

Current printing (last digit):
10 9 8 7 6 5 4 3 2

Printed in the United States of America

CONTENTS

iv   CONTENTS

CONTRIBUTORS

ROBERT Z. ALIBER, Professor of Economics, Graduate School of Business, University of Chicago

SVEN W. ARNDT, Professor of Economics, University of California, Santa Cruz

MARCELLO DE CECCO, Professor of Economics, University of Siena

GORDON K. DOUGLASS, Chairman, Department of Economics, Pomona College

J. MARCUS FLEMING, Senior Adviser, Research Department, International Monetary Fund

ISAIAH FRANK, William L. Clayton Professor of International Economics, School of Advanced International Studies, The Johns Hopkins University

SVEN GRASSMAN, Research Fellow, Stockholm Institute for International Economic Studies

GOTTFRIED HABERLER, Galen L. Stone Professor of International Trade Emeritus, Harvard University; Resident Scholar, American Enterprise Institute

RANDALL HINSHAW, Professor of Economics, Claremont Graduate School

CONRAD C. JAMISON, Vice President and Economist, Security Pacific National Bank

STEVEN W. KOHLHAGEN, University of California, Berkeley

ARTHUR B. LAFFER, Consultant to the Secretary of the Treasury; the Economist, U. S. Office of Management and Budget, 1970-72

H. C. McCLELLAN, Assistant Secretary of Commerce for International Affairs, 1955-57

RONALD I. McKINNON, Professor of Economics, Stanford University

ROBERT W. OLIVER, Professor of Economics, California Institute of Technology

Lord ROBBINS (Moderator), Chairman, Court of Governors, The London School of Economics and Political Science

WALTER S. SALANT, Senior Fellow, The Brookings Institution

WILSON E. SCHMIDT, Chairman, Department of Economics, Virginia Polytechnic Institute and State University

TIBOR SCITOVSKY, Professor of Economics, Stanford University

LEONARD S. SILK, Editorial Board, The New York Times

EGON SOHMEN, Professor of Economics, University of Heidelberg

ROBERT SOLOMON, Adviser to the Board, Board of Governors of the Federal Reserve System

FRANK M. TAMAGNA, Professor of Economics, The American University; international economic adviser

WILLARD L. THORP (Chairman), Assistant Secretary of State for Economic Affairs, 1947-52

ROBERT TRIFFIN, Frederick William Beinecke Professor of Economics, Yale University

HENRY C. WALLICH, Governor, Board of Governors of the Federal Reserve System

MARINA v. N. WHITMAN, Member, President's Council of Economic Advisers, 1972-73; Distinguished Public Service Professor of Economics, University of Pittsburgh

THOMAS D. WILLETT, Deputy Assistant Secretary of the Treasury

ARTHUR N. YOUNG, international economic adviser

JOHN PARKE YOUNG, former Chief, Division of International Finance, U. S. Department of State

FOREWORD

In a rapidly deteriorating economic setting, made much worse
by a drastic increase in the price of oil, thirty economists—including some of the most distinguished in the world—gathered in
Claremont in March 1975 to discuss "International Aspects of the
World Economic Crisis." The New York Times, in reporting
the conference, carried the headline, "World Depression? Economists Find One Now Going On." Unemployment in the United
States had reached the highest rate in more than three decades,
but, in radical contrast to the situation during the Great Depression, the growing unemployment was accompanied, not by falling
prices, but by "double-digit" inflation. Though both the unemployment and the inflation have since moderated, the problem
has by no means disappeared; indeed, "stagflation" remains the
most baffling economic problem of the 1970s—a problem which,
because of unwanted side effects, does not respond satisfactorily
to traditional remedies, whether classical or Keynesian. This
topic became the central theme of the 1975 Claremont meeting.

The present-tense quality of the subject under discussion has
been characteristic of the biennial sessions ever since they began at the Johns Hopkins University Center in Bologna in 1967.
At each of the four preceding conferences, the topic was as current as the latest news: the price of gold; international adjustment; global inflation; and international monetary reform.

All the conferences (two in Europe, three in California) have
been completely flexible dialogues. Good-humored and gentle
regulation by the Chairman, Willard L. Thorp (in all five

conferences), and by the Moderator, Lord Robbins (in all but one), kept the flow of ideas brisk and the direction reasonably constant.

Randall Hinshaw of Claremont Graduate School, the organizer, planning chairman, and rapporteur for all five conferences, has produced a book such as this one from each. The volumes were distilled from tape recordings of the sessions by an exacting process that has kept the wisdom, spontaneity, and wit of the dialogue. Professor Hinshaw wisely has never counted the hours of transcribing and editing that he has invested in each of these books.

What do these conferences and books accomplish? Chairman Thorp said in his opening remarks at one session, ". . . there is no doubt in my mind that discussions among experts, including some in positions of special responsibility, cannot help but move us on toward solutions." Years ago, the late historian, Carl Lotus Becker, wrote a statement that also seems pertinent to these dialogues: "Economic distress will teach men, if anything can, that realities are less dangerous than fancies and that fact-finding is more effective than fault-finding."

Claremont Graduate School is indebted for the success of the 1975 conference to more individuals than could be listed in this foreword. They range from members of the planning committee to the considerable number of students who provided local transportation for the conference members. Two institutions, however, deserve special thanks: The John Randolph Haynes and Dora Haynes Foundation and Security Pacific National Bank, which, with equal contributions, provided the entire financial support for the conference.

Claremont Graduate School conducted the conference with the cooperation of the other Claremont Colleges—in particular, Scripps College, on whose campus the meeting took place.

JOSEPH B. PLATT
President
Claremont Graduate School

I. INTRODUCTION

Randall Hinshaw

For the fifth time since 1967, a group of eminent economists met in March 1975 for a "freewheeling dialogue" on international monetary issues. As at all the preceding biennial meetings, the Chair was occupied by Willard L. Thorp, aptly described by one member as "the greatest expert in the chairmanship of conferences in the Western world." Lord Robbins served as Moderator, delivering at the opening session the only formal address of the conference and, as the final item on the agenda, offering a characteristically judicious critical summary of the dialogue. The meeting took place in Claremont, California under the auspices of Claremont Graduate School; two of the preceding four conferences had been held in Bologna, Italy under the auspices of the Johns Hopkins University Bologna Center.

Since the conference of February 1973, two international developments had occurred which had profoundly altered the international economic environment: the breakdown of the Bretton Woods system of pegged exchange rates and the drastic increase in the price of oil imposed by the OPEC countries. The first development meant that, for better or worse, international monetary reform — the theme of the 1973 conference — had been, to use Robert Solomon's words, "put on a back burner." The second development involved both a substantial redistribution of world income in favor of the OPEC countries and, directly or indirectly, a major contribution to global inflation.

The announced theme of the 1975 conference was "International Aspects of the World Economic Crisis." In retrospect, "crisis"

1

may appear to have been too strong a word.   But it did not seem
so at the time—particularly with respect to the United States,
which had not yet reached the bottom of by far the steepest recession since World War II.   Unemployment had been increasing rapidly since the spring of 1974 and, two months after the
conference, was to reach 9.2 percent.   To make matters much
more serious, this development had been accompanied throughout 1974 by "double-digit" inflation; the U.S. consumer-price
index had risen at an annual rate of 11-13 percent during every
quarter of that year.   Thus the problem of "stagflation"—the
coexistence of unemployment and inflation—had emerged in an
acute form.   Although a far from beautiful word, the term suc-
cinctly identifies the foremost economic problem of the 1970s
and, despite competition from a few semantic contenders (e.g.,
"slumpflation," "inflession"), has come into widespread use
as a means of avoiding tiresome circumlocution.

This problem, in its international setting, became the dominant theme of the 1975 conference.   It would be both presump-
tuous and redundant to summarize or pass judgment on the
dialogue—a task masterfully performed by Lord Robbins in his
closing critique.   In the light of subsequent events, however, a
few broad generalizations may be in order.

First, of course, the problem of stagflation, though in a
somewhat less acute form, is still very much with us.   That
problem, as Gottfried Haberler pointed out, confronts those in
power with an exasperating dilemma: efforts to reduce unemployment are likely to increase inflation, while efforts to reduce
inflation are likely to increase unemployment.   In such a setting,
neither classical nor Keynesian remedies appear to work in a
satisfactory manner.

The possibility of such a dilemma was not completely overlooked by Keynes.   The expansionary fiscal and monetary remedies prescribed in The General Theory of Employment, Interest, and Money had been designed, of course, to deal with the
massive unemployment associated with the Great Depression.
Under conditions of generalized unemployment of men and equipment, Keynes had argued, such remedies would increase employment without significantly raising prices.   But Keynes was
quick to recognize (in Chapter 21 of The General Theory) that,
as the limits of existing productive capacity were approached,
bottlenecks—at first in isolated sectors and later more generally—would appear and that, possibly long before the attainment
of full employment, prices might rise at an uncomfortable rate.

Although Keynes did not stress the point—after all, he was writing during a period of painful deflation—he clearly implied that there could be a broad range within which a country might have the worst of two worlds: under the influence of expansionary Keynesian policies, it could be experiencing sharply rising prices while still suffering from severe unemployment.

But Keynes, a firm believer in "money illusion" (at least under conditions of deep depression), did not foresee the phenomenon of "cost-push" inflation, in which rising prices induce wage settlements far in excess of any increase in the productivity of labor—and often far in excess of any current rise in the cost of living. Thus, in technical language, the problem of the 1970s is not merely that the Keynesian "aggregate supply function" is J-shaped in the short run as full employment is approached but that, because of cost-push influences, the function itself shifts persistently upward at a disturbing rate. Under such conditions, stagflation can be elegantly explained within a Keynesian framework, but the traditional Keynesian remedies would appear to be ineffective in coping with the basic dilemma described by Haberler—unless a country is prepared to settle for some bleak and unstable "trade-off" between unemployment and inflation.

In this connection, the international developments alluded to earlier have added substantially in certain countries to the severity of inflation, unemployment, or both. The cost-push influence of the oil-price increase is obvious. Of course, as some economists are fond of pointing out, a price increase in one sector does not necessarily imply an increase in the price level, since (assuming a given money supply) more money spent on one commodity leaves less money to be spent on others. Thus, if prices are flexible in both directions, a price increase in one sector may be offset by price reductions elsewhere. But this argument assumes that the money supply is not increasing (or, more precisely, that it is not increasing more rapidly than real output). Actually, of course, in such an extreme case as the quintupling of the oil price, the political and social pressures to increase the money supply at an excessive rate have for many countries been all but irresistible because of the understandable desire to avoid the unemployment that would otherwise occur. And, as Professor Kohlhagen observed at the conference, mere halfway measures of monetary expansion in such a situation may simply result in stagflation—that is, may produce or add to inflation without preventing a state of affairs in which unemployment becomes a serious problem.

A similar observation can be made about the breakdown of the Bretton Woods system of pegged exchange rates. For countries with depreciating currencies (for example, currencies which are depreciating because of rising payments for foreign oil), there is an additional cost-push element—namely, rising prices for several categories of goods: for imports, for domestic goods made from imported raw materials, for domestic goods competing with imports, and—often overlooked—for "exportables," a large fraction of which may be consumed at home. Dollar depreciation, which actually began on an important scale in mid-1970 with the appreciation of the Canadian dollar (roughly one-fourth of U. S. foreign trade is with Canada), was a major influence in boosting U. S. costs and prices during the early 1970s, just as sterling depreciation has been an even more important influence in the double-digit inflation suffered by the United Kingdom.

Of course, currency depreciation is a proximate rather than an ultimate cause of rising prices; the depreciation itself has to be explained, and may be due to external influences, such as the oil-price increase, or may be due to excessively expansionary domestic policies. In either case, the depreciation may be exacerbated by outflows of "hot money." But, whatever the ultimate cause, currency depreciation has direct effects on the depreciating country's price level; some of the price increases are immediate, and some occur with lags which may range from a few weeks to many months. And to the extent that such price increases lead to excessive wage boosts, the price level may continue moving briskly upward long after the currency depreciation has ceased.

To leave matters here, however, would not be entirely fair. As has already been noted, countries are exposed to both external and internal inflationary influences, and for those countries which have been more successful than others in resisting domestic temptations to inflate, the new regime of flexible exchange rates, by permitting currencies to appreciate, has undoubtedly reduced external inflationary pressures. This is a great virtue of exchange-rate flexibility and one not lightly to be dismissed.

At the same time, one can still be uneasy about the net inflationary impact of the new international monetary system (or "nonsystem," to quote Professor Mundell). For one thing, in the modern industrial world, both for countries whose currencies

are depreciating and for countries whose currencies are appreciating, wages are flexible in one direction only; they are
free to move up but not to move down. This means that, for
reasons already noted, costs and prices rise in the depreciating countries without tending to fall in the appreciating countries. Under such conditions, the net effect on world prices
of exchange-rate flexibility—when measured in a currency
which is neither depreciating nor appreciating—is clearly
upward.

But one can also be uneasy about the inflationary impact of
the new arrangements from another point of view. One of the
alleged virtues of flexible exchange rates is that they reduce
the need for international monetary reserves; indeed, under a
regime of completely uncontrolled floating, reserves would no
longer be used at all. But, of course, the regime which replaced the Bretton Woods arrangements has been anything but
a system of freely floating exchange rates. Some currencies
have remained more or less pegged to the dollar, others to
sterling, and still others—notably certain Common Market
currencies—to each other. Central bank intervention in the
foreign-exchange market has been frequent both by countries
having certain pegging objectives and by countries having no
such aims. But, whatever the need for international monetary
reserves, the global total has continued to rise briskly under
the new exchange-rate regime. Measured in SDRs, world
reserves rose by 18 percent in 1974, by 8 percent in 1975, and
by 13 percent in 1976. Except for 1975, these are double-digit
growth rates, and one wonders what the effects have been on
domestic economic policy. They have certainly not been deflationary.

So much for personal observations, some of which have the
unfair advantage of hindsight. Like other books in the series,
this volume, apart from the introduction, is a lightly edited
transcript of the conference tape recording. Conference members were given an opportunity to review their statements, but
were asked not to polish their conversational style and, in particular, not to change the sense of what they had said (economists have been known to change their minds). Members were,
of course, permitted to suppress statements they had made, but
none did so. All traces of wit and humor have been retained,
and no effort has been made to remove slang or colorful ex-
pressions (though in one case initials were substituted for the
expression actually used). As always, the contributors were

most cooperative, and are hereby heartily thanked.

The opening address of Lord Robbins is presented in Chapter II. This is followed in Chapter III by a general exchange of views, led by Robert Solomon, on current issues. Based on these opening statements, the conference agenda embraces four broad topics, each providing the content of a chapter of the book. Chapter IV is a review, led by Robert Triffin, of current international monetary developments — in particular, the experience with flexible exchange rates — to determine their bearing on the twin problems of inflation and unemployment. Introduced by Arthur Laffer, Chapter V is an exploration of the nature and causes of stagflation in both a domestic and an international context. Chapter VI, introduced by Isaiah Frank, is a dialogue on the relation to stagflation of the oil-price increase and of possible similar cartel behavior by producers of other commodities. Chapter VII, with an opening statement by Leonard Silk, examines domestic and international economic issues in the longer run. The book ends with the summary and critique of Lord Robbins.

II. BACKGROUND AND ANALYSIS

Lord Robbins

Chairman WILLARD L. THORP: This is our fifth conference, and it is interesting to note how little repetition there has been other than in membership. Actually, more than eighty economists have participated at these meetings, most of them having attended more than one. The topics have all related to international monetary matters, but each biennium has produced a new focal point for discussion.

The 1967 conference—and it seems very far away now—centered on the problem of gold, a subject which still is of interest to many people. At that time, we had not only the normal group of economists but also a number of "gold bugs": Jacques Rueff, a delegation from South Africa, and John Exter with his "inverted pyramid." The second conference, in 1969, came at a time when there was growing concern about exchange-rate policy and international adjustment. What we did, therefore, was to have a discussion about questions relating to the exchange-rate system— fixed rates, flexible rates, crawling pegs, wider bands—all the possible variations one could think of in order to deal more effectively with problems of international adjustment. Of all our meetings, this came nearest to what one might call a highly technical conference.

The appearance of inflation as a world problem—and sometimes we forget that the problem goes back to the beginning of this decade—was the subject of our 1971 meeting. Among other things, we discussed the question of whether Eurodollars, as an uncontrolled element in the world economy, were contributing

greatly to global inflation. When we came to the fourth conference in 1973, we were confronted with what we thought of as a
crisis. There had been, just before, two devaluations of the
dollar, and we concentrated on issues in international monetary
reform at a time when much thinking on this subject was going
on in high official circles.

I'm sorry I can't report that at any of these conferences there
was total agreement. Probably the main thing that happened was
that there was at least more understanding about why we seemed
to disagree. At any rate, we did get a great deal of stimulating
benefit through the exchange of knowledge about history and about
certain specific facts and relationships that had emerged from
research by this or that participant. I would say that, looking
back over the record, the previous four conferences would be
regarded, as conferences go, as highly successful, and of course
we are here today to carry on that tradition.

When we come to the present conference, we have to realize
that each subject which we have discussed in the past is still
with us. The last meeting of the International Monetary Fund
devoted considerable attention to gold, for example; and we have
a de facto rather than a de jure international monetary system,
still unreformed. We have a monetary structure beset by an
inflation quite different in dimension from the inflation in progress when we discussed this topic before. Moreover, the inflation is now proceeding in a setting of severe world recession.
At the time of all our earlier conferences, there had not been
even a mild recession which might have led us to consider that
as an aspect of international monetary problems. Apart from
these matters, there is the OPEC problem with all its ramifica-
tions and implications for the future. Finally, the disequilibria
among countries in their balances of payments are of record-
breaking size.

So it is clear that the problems today are of greater than
usual gravity, and are worldwide. This is no time for fun and
games or for economics and politics as usual. On the contrary, we are confronted with the greatest challenge since this
series of conferences began. And now the time has come to
consider more specifically what we want to talk about together.
As you all know, we have a traditional approach to this task. If
I may paraphrase the description of a beginning long ago, I
would say, "In the beginning, there was chaos, and then there
was Lionel Robbins!" After his broad review of our topic, I
hope that a number of you will suggest what the priorities should

be among the subjects we might usefully discuss in our later
sessions. Lord Robbins:

Lord ROBBINS: Thank you, Willard, for those extremely
embarrassing words. I am acutely aware that the conclusion
reached by our members, when I have finished my observations,
will be that I have made chaos more chaotic. I am also acutely
aware that I share some responsibility with Randall Hinshaw for
the choice of a title for our conference theme, so perhaps I ought
to confess that, on sitting down to prepare these remarks, I felt
a tinge of contrition.

After all, "crisis" is a very strong word indeed, and it may
be too strong a description of the economic condition of the
world—as distinct from the political condition, where, I think,
the word is strictly applicable, as it has been since 1945. I am
pretty sure that the word crisis applies to the economic condition of my own unfortunate country, the United Kingdom—once
so stable, but now dominated by ideas which have gone all soft
and silly.

But I am not so sure about affairs elsewhere. I agree with
you, Willard, that there are unmistakable signs of depression,
but I have little doubt that, let us say, by the middle of 1976
there may be some signs of emergence—if not something better
than that—and that progress and prosperity will once more return
to this admirable Union. In continental Europe, while there are
serious problems, particularly in Italy, I would not call the present situation, at least on the economic side, a state of crisis.
The oil countries are certainly doing very well. As to the rest,
apart from India, where the menace of overpopulation grows
yearly greater, I submit that generalization is absurd. There
is much that is cause for concern in the condition of the so-called
underdeveloped countries, but overall crisis is perhaps a misleading terminology. And I leave out of account the totalitarian
world, whose aims and criteria are so different from our own as
to make the use of a common language almost meaningless.

Nevertheless, after this slightly protracted apologia, I do submit that there is plenty for us to talk about. If the word crisis
is too strong, it would be difficult to argue that the present state
of affairs, viewed in the large, is one of normal stability. In
the industrialized countries, there are higher rates of inflation
than have often occurred in peacetime history. At the same
time—and this makes the situation unusual—these brisk rates
of inflation are accompanied by various degrees of depression

and slack use of resources. As Willard pointed out, there is
no longer any orderly relationship between the various currencies. There is much fear of instability in the international
capital markets. And there is the change in the price of oil
which, whatever its ultimate significance, is the cause of a
great many headaches and apprehensions.

So here we are in this paradisaical spot, without any excuse
for not filling every moment with deliberations on matters which,
if not to be described as crises, are yet of great importance to
the future of free societies. My job, as Willard said, is simply
to indicate—under the headings which you may have noticed I
have surreptitiously introduced already—some of the questions
on which clear and judicious pronouncements might be valuable.

I

Let me begin with inflation. I won't dwell at this stage on
the different rates of inflation which prevail in different parts
of the world; that I shall deal with later. I am concerned rather
with inflation as a general phenomenon—a common feature of
the free-world situation, a state of affairs which in some degree
has been prevalent in the last thirty years, but recently at a much
smarter pace.

Now it is common ground among competent economists that
an excess of expenditure over the value of production at constant
prices—which is one way of defining inflation—cannot take place
for long if there is no increase in the supply of money in the
broad sense of the word. I know of no one who would deny the
influence of changes in velocity of demand—whatever way you
care to put it—but few, I think, would contend that, in the medium term, changes of this sort are likely to have a dominating
influence if the rate of increase in the supply of money does not
exceed the limits I have mentioned. It follows, I think, that
whatever the initiating cause—interest rates low in relation to
profit expectations, government or private expenditure, or demands for increases of income exceeding the prospective rates
of increase of productivity—it is a necessary condition (I choose
my words deliberately) for the continuation of inflation that an
increase of money supply should sustain these tendencies.

The idea that there can be continuing inflation at the rates
recently prevailing in Western countries without such movements
in money supply seems to me to be inherently improbable. Where
expert opinion still differs in this respect seems to me, although

not to everybody, to be a matter of semantics. Because, in the last analysis, governments and central banks control the supply of money, there is a certain school of thought—represented on a very exalted plane by my dear friend, Milton Friedman, and on a much lower plane in my country by Mr. Enoch Powell— which argues that the sole responsibility for inflation is governmental and that any talk of inflation originating on the side of cost is misleading. Needless to say, this diagnosis is highly congenial to bodies of organized producers. I must say that I find this way of putting things either highly sophisticated in the case of Professor Friedman or highly simplistic in the case of Mr. Powell.

Of course we should all agree that a relative increase of money supply is an essential condition of inflation. But if one is to talk at all of initiating causes—and a self-denying ordinance in that respect is rather absurd—we must go further. If we have governments committed to policies of full employment and the trade unions demand, and are conceded, increases of pay, as in my country, often several times the increase in their productivity, and if, in such circumstances, governments perhaps weakly allow the money supply to increase to finance the process, it does seem to me to be paradoxical to say that there is no meaning in statements which assign some of the causation of inflation to this sort of monopolistic pressure. I have heard it said— indeed, I heard Milton say it himself a few weeks ago—that, in any case, wage demands have a once-for-all impact, whereas inflation is a continuing process. Well, on this, with all affection and Christian charity, I can only say that I wish Milton and his friends would prolong their highly valuable visits to the United Kingdom, because it might enlarge their conception of appetites which grow by feeding.

Now a word about cures. It is sometimes urged that this dreadful scourge could be eliminated, or at least diminished, by the device which nowadays goes by the horrid name of "indexation." That is to say, if various contracts and tax obligations could be linked to changes in the value of money—in essence, if we were to adopt the Tabular Standard recommended by Stanley Jevons nearly a hundred years ago—then we should be well on our way to curbing these disturbing tendencies. Now let me say at once that I am not, repeat not, opposed to indexation in many circumstances. The state of affairs in which, because of inflation, groups of people who have already suffered in that way are dragged into higher tax brackets is surely manifestly unjust,

however agreeable it may be to impoverished ministers of
finance. And, further, I would argue that if, in a growing economy—and please notice the word growing—wages and salaries
are so linked, then clearly we should be on the way to elimi-
nating some of the worst evils of inflation. Good work, perhaps,
has been done in certain Latin American countries in that respect.
And let me say as a matter of stratospheric theory that of course
I should agree that if everything, including bank balances, were
indexed, then inflation on the money side would lose all meaning; it would simply be a matter of changing all the figures in
all the books.

But of course we are not likely to go that way. To destroy
the power to put extra purchasing power in the hands of governments or pressure groups would be a policy which would encounter very strong resistance. But I have a much more down-to-
earth and practical observation. Indexation is all very well as
a means of saving certain important groups from changes in the
value of money arising from changes on the money side. But
what about adverse changes on the goods side? Suppose that, in
a closed economy, there is an earthquake or a drought which
causes the "T" in the old Fisher equation to shrink against a
constant "M"; in that case, the result will surely be a rise in
price caused by a falling off in the flow of goods. Indeed, it is
a condition of equilibrium in such circumstances that such a
falling off must be reflected in real incomes. I submit that, in
such circumstances, an index which ties money incomes to a
price index is a positively destabilizing factor; it is a recipe for
built-in inflation. My example was specifically chosen to relate
to a closed economy in order not to arouse too much controversy
at this stage. But let me ask at this stage how different my example is from the state of affairs which arises on the goods side in
an open economy if there are adverse changes in the terms
of trade.

II

So much by way of preliminary observation on inflation as a
general phenomenon. I now come to the second matter I want
to ventilate: the coexistence of depression and inflation. I take
it that we should all agree that a diminution of the rate of increase
of money supply is likely to cause some degree of depression.
Further, we should agree that the rise in money rates of interest
which accompanies growing realization on the part of the public

that they are being fooled—that, owing to inflation, real rates
of interest are much lower than money rates, or even negative—
is likely to cause difficulties in the financial markets of the
world and a slowing up of investment. We also know that accounting practices, owing to the time lag in the habits of that
extremely honorable profession—practices which assume constant prices in estimating appropriate depreciation quotas—tend
to lead to a relative diminution of real working capital as inflation proceeds, and this in turn is unfavorable to continued
prosperity.

All these tendencies have shown themselves in the course of
recent developments. What is novel in the present position, in
some countries at least, is the persistence of inflation when
these depressing influences have become operative. Slump
combined with continuing inflation—at any rate, before inflation
becomes hyperinflation—has not been a frequent conjunction in
history, and its occurrence at the present time certainly presents something of a problem. Now it is possible that part of
the explanation may be found by the recognition of time lags
which we are all too apt to omit in consideration of these subjects. We know that inflationary tendencies take time to work
themselves out. The inflation which is going merrily ahead in
the United Kingdom is certainly due in part to policies which
were initiated by the Conservative government in earlier years.
But I doubt that time lags furnish the whole story. In some
countries—at any rate, in the United Kingdom—I am inclined
to attribute some of the persistence of inflation to continuing
influences on the side of cost, which the commitment to high
levels of employment has failed sufficiently to curb.

Be that as it may, the question certainly presents itself how
the continuing inflation can be restrained. And this at once
raises the problem of direct control of incomes—so-called incomes policy—a matter discussed before at these conferences.
Personally, looking back at what I've said in the past on this
subject, I find nothing that I wish to retract. Indeed, experience in Great Britain strongly reinforces my conviction that in
the long run—and I emphasize the words "in the long run"—such
policies have a very slim chance of success. Our experience
makes it abundantly clear that, although very fashionable some
years ago, the idea that there can be pursued a policy of high-
pressure demand to maintain ultra-full employment, and at the
same time a policy of central regulation of incomes to restrain
inflation, simply does not work. The inflation eventually sweeps

aside the inflation controls; it carries with it pressures which the controls are unable to resist.

But now I wish to say something further on the matter. Having, I hope, made my position clear on the long-term prospect, I should like to add that I can conceive of situations in which restraints on incomes can be of temporary assistance. Suppose that governments and central banks are taking steps to reduce the rate of increase of money supply and the rate of increase of public expenditure, and suppose that at the same time the trade unions and other such bodies are still putting forward claims far exceeding the increase in the value of their product. In such circumstances, I don't find it impossible to conceive that a temporary freeze or regulation of wage increases may prevent some of the unemployment which would have occurred had the claims been successful. That is to say, conceived in this way, a temporary incomes policy is to be regarded, not as a restraint on inflation, but rather as a substitute for the unemployment which might otherwise have occurred while the excess expenditure is being diminished.

I would not expect such regulation to be viable for any but short periods, nor would I be at all sanguine that such a policy would have a chance of being adopted. Hitherto in history, incomes policies have provided the pretext for avoiding reductions of inflationary expenditure rather than mitigating the effect of such reductions. But I don't think that the possibility should be ruled out. I would simply emphasize that one could expect it to be successful only for a short time and that if, prior to the time the otherwise inevitable breakdown comes, the fundamental inflationary influences are not eliminated, it would not have fulfilled its purpose.

III

Up to this point, I have been discussing problems common to most parts of the free world—inflation and the coexistence of inflation with depression. I now turn to problems which arise from the absence of common policies in the free world as a whole—in particular, problems which arise from the absence of a common monetary unit, or, putting the matter more realistically, problems which arise from the existence of different moneys, of different monetary and financial policies, and the various disturbances to which this state of affairs gives rise.

Now let me say at once, unashamedly—with Gottfried Haberler within five yards of me—that I am fundamentally a common-
money man in this sense: that I regard money-changing as an
interruption of spontaneous economic intercourse. I regard the
existence of exchange markets ideally as merely a by-product
of the existence of separate political units having sovereign
powers as regards the management of money—sovereign powers
which I submit no sensible person would wish to see brought into
existence if they didn't exist already. I wonder if any of you
present would like to see independent currencies and independent monetary policies in each of the fifty states of the Union.
Surely, the reductio ad absurdum to such a state of affairs is
simply the elimination of a medium of exchange—a reversion
to a state of barter. And, politics apart, the apologia for areas
having different monetary units, in the last sophisticated analysis, is that, in circumstances in which the terms of trade turn
against an area, the relative reduction in real incomes can be
made more expeditiously by changes in rates of exchange than
by changes in money incomes. This, I submit in all affection
and friendliness, is an odd argument for money illusion on the
part of theoretical democrats. But I don't deny that sometimes
it has down-to-earth practical significance.

Personally, I have little doubt that if it were not for political
restraints which nowadays we've grown so used to that we take
them as being part of the order of nature, a common money or
the equivalent of a common money would fairly speedily establish itself. Who among us, knowing the present state of the
world, would not wish to be paid in a strong currency rather
than a weak one? Surely, it is only the explicit political pro-
hibition, doubtless with some practical justification, which
prevents that sort of thing happening on a larger scale today.
Perhaps we're different in Great Britain, but I cannot think of
any British economist—and, as you know, British economists
quarrel like Kilkenney cats—who, whatever his views on public
policy, would not prefer to have his pay and pension fixed in
marks rather than in sterling. And let me remind you—Gottfried
will remember this, but most of you are too young—that this sort
of thing spread like wildfire in central Europe during the inflations of the 1920s, before people had invented limitations on gold
clauses in commercial contracts or on the holding of foreign currencies without permission.

But now let's come down to earth. History has left its deposit
in the shape of existing political structures. Those who rule

over us have eaten of the fruit of the Tree of Knowledge to this
extent: that they realize that by these expedients their position
is fortified and that, given the existence of a common money,
their freedom of maneuver would be tremendously curtailed.
And so, whatever may happen in the future, we have to deal
here and now with a world in which there are many different
centers of manufacture of money and credit, with quite ferocious
penalties for those who try to safeguard their position by opting
out of local transactions in terms of local money. And if any
of you think this is a new idea, let me implore you to read the
passages in Plato's Laws in which he recommends first a value-
less internal currency and then penalties almost amounting to
death for those who, having been given permission to take metallic currency abroad on their travels, fail to return it—and even
for those who don't inform on their friends whom they know to
have a few gold or silver coins in their possession.

Now lest you think that these reflections have been leading up
to some exhortation to impose definitely fixed parities on currencies whose relative values as a result of either external or internal influences are changing—lest you think I have that up my
sleeve—let me say at once that I am still a good Bretton Woods
man (I happen to be one of the few survivors) in the sense that,
recognizing the possibilities of the present political structure
of the world, I am in favor of movable parities. I should also
like to say—and here I am trying to vindicate myself vis-a-vis
Gottfried—that if it were desired for some reason (the unifica-
tion of Europe, for instance) to amalgamate certain local currencies, I should be very much against immediately clamping
things down to a Procrustean bed of fixed parities without some
period of experimentation to discover whether, in particular
circumstances, there was undervaluation or overvaluation. So
I daresay that the observations I am going to make will not commend themselves to many of you here present. But these observations do not spring from belief in fixity where, as the result
of the absence of common control, there is disequilibrium, nor
from any desire to impose fixity at the present moment where
fixity would be disequilibrating.

But having said that—with only faint hope of avoiding misunderstanding—let me make certain tentative observations on
the present state of affairs. First of all, let me observe that,
whatever may be our judgment on what has happened since the
breakup of the Smithsonian agreement, it does not begin to
approximate to the ideal, cherished by so many of my friends

with whom I would love to agree but don't, of absolute free
floating all around. I've said before, and I say it again, that
if we were to have floating without some supranational control,
it will be dirty floating rather than clean; and nothing that has
happened since we last discussed these matters leads me to
retract this proposition. Members of the conference, why do
leading statesmen and central bankers fly around in airplanes,
pleading support for this currency or that, if they are not pursuing policies which keep the market values of these currencies
different from what they would have been otherwise? I'm not
blaming the poor politicians for doing this; it springs from their
natural impulses. I'm merely pointing out that it happens. And,
having regard to the fact that some fluctuation which otherwise
would have taken place might upset the apple cart for them as
regards internal arrangements, giving rise to demands for increased wages and so on, it is not difficult to understand, or
even to sympathize with, the motives which lead to these extensive travels. In any case, I submit that if there is to be floating
in the world we live in, dirty floating is going to be the order
of the day.

The second observation that I should like to make in this
connection is this: that the absence of commonly agreed rates
has its dangers as well as some advantages. Now I'm not deny-
ing the advantages. In the present inflationary madness of some
parts of the world, freedom to appreciate the rate of exchange
is a very useful method of avoiding the importation of other
people's inflation. The West German Republic, insofar as its
government has submitted to the somewhat unorthodox proceeding, has gained considerably in this way.

But equally, there are dangerous possibilities. The unprece-
dented and well-nigh catastrophic inflation from which the United
Kingdom is now suffering was certainly stoked up by measures
introduced by a Chancellor of the Exchequer—incidentally a very
nice man—who explicitly rejoiced in the fact that, since the
pound had broken free from its international commitment, there
was no need to worry about the effects on the foreign exchanges
of internal policy. It may seem to some of you a dreadful thing
to say, but I think it is arguable that the different rates of inflation have become much steeper since the virtual abandonment
of attempts to maintain some sort of predictable relationship
between key currencies. Since I have spoken of one Chancellor
of the Exchequer, I might speak of another; I can't forbear to
draw attention to the odd spectacle of the minister of a once

important country going around to various capitals, himself
worried about inflation, exhorting others to inflate in order to
avert for him the disagreeable consequences of inflation in his
own country. And surely it should be a matter for common
agreement that if, for good reasons, an exchange rate is allowed
to fall, then, for the time being at any rate, there is need for a
stiffer internal monetary policy if the initial fall is not to initiate
a sort of cumulative Wicksellian process which itself calls for
further depreciation.

To conclude this part of my observations on the absence of
any international order as regards currencies, I would like to
draw attention to a very considerable instability of the international capital market which goes with this absence of order. I
would agree—I hope this will preserve for me some sort of sem-
blance of toleration—that if it were a matter of consensus regarding wider margins, or greater freedom of action within
these margins, such a state of affairs might actually be an aid
to stabilization in providing greater elbowroom for dealing with
unjustifiable speculation. But present conditions are far from
that, and the prevalence of vast volumes of more or less free
capital—either escaped from national controls or manufactured
in spite of them, with no obvious lender of last resort and with
unlimited opportunities for dirty floating—is certainly something which must inspire anxiety.

Hitherto, I think, the central banks of the world, acting in
some sort of informal concert, have been rather clever. Recent
failures of financial institutions, which have aroused disagreeable recollections of similar collapses in the interwar period,
seem to have been reasonably well contained. But it is not at
all clear to me that the present situation of the Eurocapital markets is such as to inspire confidence that in the event of major
trouble with a key currency—which is certainly not out of the
question—all will be well.

IV

This brings me to my last point—namely, just to touch on
some of the complications, actual and feared, of the operations
of the oil cartel. Now let me say at once that I regard with the
deepest apprehension the operations of this body insofar as they
have a political aspect. Indeed, I agree with the President of
the United States that an almost intolerable situation is created
if the economic activities of the greater part of the free world

can be paralyzed for the purpose of forcing diplomatic pressure for the settlement of disputes between Middle Eastern communities.   I am surprised how quickly people can forget what has happened in this respect and how readily many appear to be willing to be swayed by this kind of pressure.   But we are here to discuss economic problems rather than political, and I don't wish to allow myself to expatiate further on that aspect of the matter — though I must say that for me it entirely outweighs any of the other problems arising in this respect.

As regards the economic aspects, there are several things to say.   First, a truism.   Unquestionably involved is a transfer of wealth between the rest of the world and the cartel.   Now, considering this matter calmly, I can't believe that, as regards the industrial countries, this is an insupportable burden.   Assuming very moderate rates of growth per annum, at worst the statistical necessities of transfer don't involve much more than a retreat to the living standards, let us say, of the late 1960s, which were not intolerable.   For the poorer parts of the world, of course, it is a much more serious question.

Secondly, taking the free world as a whole and assuming no other disturbing factors, to the extent that the price rise is sustained by output lower than otherwise would have been the case, it must mean lower relative production against relative expenditure.   Now whether you call this inflationary or not is a semantic question, depending on how you define inflation.   If inflation is defined as any volume of money in relation to goods which allows a fall in the value of money, then you have inflation.   But all this is so far from reality that it is not very important.   What in the present condition of opinion is much more likely is that, instead of the rest of the world having less to spend on things other than oil, the various governmental authorities will endeavor to offset the deprivation of purchasing power by creating more — and that clearly will be inflationary.   Whatever we may blame the Arabs for, it would be difficult to blame them for that.

Having said this, I should like to add that I am not unaware of the problem which exercises men's minds about what is going to happen as a result of the transfer.   To this, I take it, the general answer must be the entirely banal proposition that it all depends.   If the wealth that is transferred is spent by the OPEC countries on additional imports or on long-term investments abroad, then, so far as the net effect on world expenditure is concerned, the result should be no change.   If, to go to the other limit, it is hoarded under the bed, then, of course, the effect on the world is deflationary. And if it is simply kept roaming about in the short-term capital market, the effect may be the creation of much potential instability and perhaps eventual crisis.

Which of these eventualities is likely to occur is, in my judgment, still a matter of great conjecture. I fancy that many people have been surprised at the increase which has already taken place in the demand for imports by the OPEC countries, although I confess I don't understand why people are surprised, because the OPEC group doesn't consist simply of Saudi Arabia and Kuwait—immensely rich centers with a very small population. There are other countries—Iraq, Iran, Nigeria, for instance— which can absorb almost any amount of money they can get hold of. So, in my judgment, some increase in the demand for imports is likely to continue.

Well, to go to the other limit again, if there were genuine hoarding by OPEC on a large and long-period scale, it is certainly not to be supposed that the governments and central banks of the world—their intellectual muscles already used to increasing the supply of money quite readily—would lack expedients to meet a general deflationary influence of that sort. But it is necessary when one is thinking about all that to remember that the rest of the world is still inflating. The real trouble will come, of course, if the transfers simply result in immense accumulations of hot money; and this may well be a genuine problem. If it materializes on the scale sometimes suggested, all the ingenuity of our financial authorities, including the Fund and the Bank, will be needed to deal with the problem. I personally hope in the course of this conference to hear of methods of dealing with this matter which are neither wishful thinking nor devices for giving Arab money away to people who would not otherwise have come into possession of it.

But now finally—and I'm nearly at the end—in making up our minds concerning the magnitude of this problem, I don't think that we should totally forget the existence of the so-called laws of supply and demand. I confess that I am perplexed when, in learned articles, bank reviews, and elsewhere, I peruse discussions of complicated financial arcana, and seldom encounter speculation concerning the effects on the supplies of oil and substitutes for oil of prices which have quadrupled in the last few years. I don't profess to be an expert on these matters—though I was once a member of an oil company—but I confess that the thought has occasionally crossed my mind that, human nature

and ingenuity being what it happily still is in most, though perhaps not all, of the countries of the free world, the OPEC group
may have overplayed its hand. The present glut of oil, although
doubtless partly due to the world recession, is at any rate a reminder that overplaying the hand may be a possibility. If that
were so, then, eventually, the transfer problem might prove
to be, like other transfer problems of past history, a matter
capable of considerable exaggeration.

Well, Mr. Chairman, I see that my time is up. I think it
could justly be said that in the course of my remarks I have
said little that is constructive and much that many of you will
regard as perverse. If that is so, the only excuse I would put
forward at this juncture is that the enumeration of problems
and the propagation of arguments is chiefly what you want me
to do.

III. DIALOGUE ON THE ISSUES

Robert Solomon and
Conference Members

Chairman THORP: Since Lord Robbins has raised a number
of problems, we should now give some thought to which of these
problems, and perhaps any additional problems, we would like
to discuss. I won't guarantee that every suggestion will be accepted. But the Chairman is going to struggle to find ways of
incorporating into the agenda as many of the suggestions as we
can hope to consider in the brief time we have together. I have
a brief list already of members who wish to make suggestions
regarding the agenda, so without further ado I shall start with
Bob Solomon.

ROBERT SOLOMON: I feel like a military volunteer at this
point, but, having forced myself on you, let me suggest three
areas on which the conference might concentrate. All three
have been touched on in one way or another in Willard's introductory remarks and in the statement of Lord Robbins.
The first point is that the world is in a recession. I suggest
that, quite apart from our concern about the loss of income and
output, which is the normal reason for opposing a recession,
there are three international reasons for being concerned.
First, there is a danger in this situation of falling output that
each country will overestimate its exports for the period ahead
and will therefore adopt counter-recessionary policies that are
inadequate. I believe that this phenomenon has already occurred
and that it helps to explain the depth and the spreading of the
recession. A second reason for being concerned is that there

23

is a tendency already visible for countries to adopt import restrictions, not only for balance-of-payments objectives, which
has happened here and there, but also for the purpose of protecting domestic employment, which has happened in Australia
and perhaps also in other countries. A third reason for concern
is that the recession in industrialized countries, occurring on
top of the increase in the price of oil and of oil-related products,
will put a very severe strain on developing countries, with all
sorts of economic, political, and social effects.

Now there was a consensus in the OECD meetings that I attended two weeks ago that the lead in pulling the world out of
this recession should be taken by the three most powerful industrial nations, which were identified as Germany, Japan, and the
United States. These countries were urged to be the leaders in
adopting counter-recessionary measures. Each had been more
successful than other countries in restraining inflation; each
had experienced a deeper contraction of output than most other
countries; and each, it was said, had less of a balance-of-payments constraint than most other countries. This doesn't mean
that other countries should not also adopt counter-recessionary
measures, but it was thought that the big push, so to speak,
should come from the big three.

With that background, I simply identify a first issue—namely,
what would be appropriate policies, including policy mixes, to
deal with world recession at a time when, as Lord Robbins has
told us, inflation is still prevalent in most countries, though
declining in some? Let me observe here that, where inflation
exists, it is not any longer an excess-demand phenomenon (at
least in industrialized countries); it's a cost-push phenomenon.

The second area on which we might focus—also mentioned
by Lord Robbins—is the impact of the oil-price rise. I view
the increase in oil prices as having exactly the same domestic
economic effects as a very stiff excise tax on petroleum, except
that this tax happens to be imposed on us by the OPEC countries, who are receiving the proceeds of the tax and are either
giving it away or lending it back to us (by "us" I mean the oil-
importing countries as a group). I believe, therefore, that the
oil-price increase has contributed to the world recession. On
the balance-of-payments side, the OPEC countries have little
choice but to give away, lend, or invest the proceeds of their
surplus with the oil-importing countries, but problems arise
in the distribution of the funds that flow back from OPEC to the
rest of the world, since that distribution may not conform to

the distribution of current-account deficits among the oil-importing countries.

Thus, one general macroeconomic question we may want to
consider is whether there should be some understandings as to
how the aggregate deficit, at least among industrialized countries, should be divided up. The deficit is inevitable for the
next few years until the world adjusts to the situation, whether
by a fall in the oil price, by a rise in OPEC imports, by a reduction in the consumption of OPEC petroleum by the rest of
the world, or by some combination of these possibilities. The
rationale for suggesting this as an issue is that unless there is
some general understanding on how the aggregate deficit among
industrialized countries should be divided up, there is a danger
that countries will adopt mutually destructive policies in trying
to pass the hot potato around. It is in order to avoid such self-
defeating policies that there is a case for thinking about mutual
understandings among countries on the division of the inevitable
aggregate current-account deficit.

Let me point out that among the policy instruments that could
be used in making such adjustments is official borrowing, which
has already become very important. This may be part of what
Lord Robbins referred to as dirty floating; these days it is often
called "managed" rather than "dirty" floating, since it is approved of by many people. But whatever one calls it, it is not
free floating. A major consequence is that official borrowing
has become an important policy instrument. It is used as an
alternative to the use of reserves, as an alternative to a movement in the exchange rate, and as an alternative to deflation as
a way of coping with the current-account deficit. The broad
question in this second area, then, is whether an attempt should
be made to allocate the deficit and the incremental debt and, if
so, what policy instruments would be appropriate.

The third issue, dealt with both by Lord Robbins and by
Willard Thorp, is the future of the international monetary system in a world of nations which, as Lord Robbins has reminded
us, are politically independent though economically interdepen-
dent. I think we are still on a dollar standard—with flexible
exchange rates, official borrowing, and some degree of intervention. Lord Robbins characterized this state of affairs as
lack of order in the international monetary system. The issue
in this third area, I would say, is whether we can, or should,
go on in this way. Are the present arrangements tolerable, or
do we need to try again to agree on a reformed system that is

more organized and coherent? Again, I am not suggesting
answers but simply trying to specify the issue. Perhaps as
a sub-issue, some of us may be interested in discussing the
question of the weakness of the dollar; why has the dollar be-
haved as it has over the past year?

GOTTFRIED HABERLER: I think the most important problem to which we ought to address ourselves is the coexistence
of inflation and stagnation—"stagflation," or "inflession," as
Robert Triffin puts it. This problem has both internal and external aspects. I don't know how much time we want to spend
on the internal aspects, but they do pose a nasty dilemma. If
we had an old-fashioned recession with falling prices, everything would be fine: spend a little more, and the falling prices
and falling output would be reversed. But the combination of
unemployment and inflation is a very different matter; if we
fight recession, we stimulate inflation, and if we fight inflation, we stimulate recession.

There is a way out, and Lord Robbins has referred to it—
namely, incomes policy. I am not going into that subject except to say that the term "incomes policy" has acquired two
distinct meanings. The usual meaning is more or less general
limitations on wage and price increases. The other meaning
is a bundle of measures designed to make an economy more
flexible and competitive. I have designated the latter kind of
policy as "Incomes Policy II," as distinguished from "Incomes
Policy I" in the conventional sense. I, personally, would accept only Incomes Policy II as a possible way out of the stagflation dilemma.

From the international standpoint, the important question
to my mind is how floating has worked and how it will work in
a recessionary climate. It is a little difficult to say what one
wants to discuss without implying how one thinks about it, but
I would say—and I could document it—that floating was simply
unavoidable. Many of the fixed-rate economists admit that.
I would say that recession makes floating even more unavoidable, but here I would like to suggest that we might go into the
question of managed and dirty floating. I myself have tried to
distinguish between merely managed floating and dirty floating; I think this is an important distinction, though it may be
a little arbitrary. I quite agree that free floating is probably
politically impossible and may not even be entirely desirable,
but dirty floating—dual exchange rates, split exchange markets, and that sort of thing—is surely avoidable, so I would

make that distinction, and perhaps we could agree on certain rules there.

This raises the question of the dollar. The dollar has been going down in the foreign-exchange markets, and many people say that the dollar is undervalued now. Is that correct? Those who say the dollar is undervalued probably mean that there has been destabilizing speculation and that we have to do something about it. That calls for managed floating.

In this connection, I would like to raise a question for possible discussion. I myself am not sure what precisely causes the dollar to go down—whether it is merely the interest differential or whether, as some say, there has been an attempt at diversification of reserves on the part of OPEC countries and other dollar holders. Now if that is an important factor—I'm not sure it is, but let us suppose it is—then one could conceive of measures that would make the diversification less of a problem. What I have in mind is to offer to foreign official dollar holders an option to have SDR-denominated securities with a lower yield. It is understandable that foreign dollar holders get nervous when they see the dollar go down, and some such arrangement for reassuring them might reduce considerably the need to diversify.

I won't say anything about the recycling of petrodollars, but if there is time a short discussion of this subject would be useful. We might also devote a little time to the role of gold in the future. Gold has been revalued, and many people are apprehensive that it may make a comeback; others, of course, want that, so perhaps a short discussion of gold matters would be in order.

MARINA v. N. WHITMAN: The big general topic that I see lurking here is really the old conflict between interdependence among countries, on the one hand, and the very strong determination to maintain national economic sovereignty, on the other. This conflict has been enhanced since World War II by the ambitious domestic economic goals to which governments have committed themselves. One can see this in the developed countries in the tension between the high degree of market integration that has taken place and the rather low degree, I would argue, of policy integration that has taken place. In the less developed countries, one can see it in the conflict between the pressure on them to specialize according to comparative advantage and their strong desire to diversify and increase their self-sufficiency.

It strikes me that one of the major arguments for flexible exchange rates concerns what one might call the dark side of interdependence — that is, the attempt to create a sort of decent distance, or greater independence, for domestic policy by means of floating rates. I think we need to explore what the outcome has been. I am struck by the fact that there seems to have been something of a convergence of opinion; the fixed-rate people admit that over the recent past fixed rates probably would have been impossible, and the flexible-rate people admit that flexible rates have not, thus far at least, brought us to Nirvana, nor are they likely to in the future. One could list — I won't do it now — the areas in which many people have experienced a certain amount of disillusionment with respect to the way flexible rates have worked. At the same time, I think many people would admit, to paraphrase Churchill, that flexible rates are the worst possible system under present conditions except for all the others. And we do need some evaluation of this experience thus far.

We also need to cast our discussion in the framework of what I like to call the new realities; I guess they're old realities which are newly recognized or newly re-recognized, one of them having to do with the fact that scarcity is real and not just the figment of the economist's imagination. What this means is that we are having, and must have, renewed emphasis on supply factors as well as on demand factors. Economic discussion, whether by Keynesians or by monetarists, has in recent history focused primarily on the demand side, and we now need to get away from the tendency to cast all our discussions in macroeconomic terms. We must have much more recourse to the messy and unsatisfactory area of microeconomics.

The second aspect of the new realities is that even the United States is part of the world and that interdependence is a two-way proposition. I suppose that what we have to face is the question of whether we are playing a zero-sum game, a positive-sum game, or possibly a negative-sum game. The basic question is whether we can actually use this interdependence to make countries as a group better off. We probably also have to face the increased fragility of public support for the market system when the pace of change becomes very rapid, and we need to discuss what one does about restoring this faith or, if restoration is impossible, what one does about that.

Getting down to specific issues, one of them quite obviously is the puzzle of why interdependence seems to have increased in a period of flexible exchange rates. Whether the floating is managed, dirty, or whatever, exchange rates are certainly much more flexible than they were before. Every textbook

tells us that flexible rates tend to bottle up disturbances inside
the countries where they originate, which means that one would
expect flexible rates to create greater divergences in economic
experience from country to country by providing this barrier
to integration. And yet the period in which we have had greater
exchange-rate flexibility has also been the period in which we
have had more synchronization than ever before, certainly of
rates of inflation, and, I believe also, of the business cycle.

We need to think about why this is so. We also need to talk
about the whole nature, under present conditions, of the international transmission mechanism both of inflation and of recession or depression. This seems to me very much of a phenomenon in search of a theory. We also need, I think, to discuss
the relationship between the transmission mechanism and the
international monetary system. At the level of abstract theory,
things should be symmetrical. Flexible rates should mean that
countries which depreciate should have higher rates of inflation
than they would under a fixed-rate system and that countries
which appreciate should have lower rates of inflation than under
a fixed-rate system, but there is no a priori reason why the
average rate of world inflation should be higher under one system than another unless there are some asymmetries in either
market responses or policy responses. I am sure those asymmetries exist, but we don't know much about them, and we need
to talk about that.

The one other point that we probably need to discuss—and I
would subsume the oil question under this—is how one mini-
mizes the disturbances to nations resulting from big changes
in relative prices and in the world distribution of income and
wealth. We don't seem to be very good at that, and we need
to talk about how we can improve our performance.

Chairman THORP: I'm sorry, but I am now going to have
to set a three-minute limit on statements, because my list is
quite long and we don't want our lunch to get cold. Bob Aliber:

ROBERT Z. ALIBER: I shall be brief. My suggestion at
this stage is that we take perspective and move back ten years.
Imagine ourselves in 1965, and recall the world as it was then—
the dollar at the center of the universe, great confidence in the
movement toward an SDR system, increasing economic and
political integration. Contrast the vision of the future that we
tended to share in 1965 with what actually happened, and ask
ourselves to what extent the sequence of events that occurred
over the past decade was the result of events over which we

had no control and to what extent that sequence reflected the policies that governments chose to follow in wisdom or in ignorance. I suggest that, as we look toward the next five or ten years, we be quite humble about our predictive ability and quite respectful of the power of governments to screw up the world.

ARTHUR B. LAFFER: Taking a cue from Marina Whitman, I would suggest that, in discussing the international aspects of world recession, we focus far more than we have in the past on the aggregate supply function of world output. I suggest that one way we should look at this matter is in relation to the very important role of taxes as a wedge between the wages that are paid and the wages that are actually received. The second major area on which I think we should concentrate is the world money supply. Taking a cue this time from Lord Robbins, we may not only have changes in velocity, as we would say in Chicago, but we also may have certain forms of money which are outside the control of the monetary authorities; I am thinking particularly of the rapid growth of Eurodollars. The third subject I think we should discuss is the general issue of changes in the terms of trade among commodities and how these changes affect trade balances, reserve levels, employment, and inflation.

J. MARCUS FLEMING: I agree with two or three speakers before me that the most important subject before us is the coincidence of depression and inflation. I have some doubts, however, about whether it would make a very good conference subject, because I have a feeling that there is too much agreement about it in the analysis. I thought that the analysis of Lord Robbins was very much of a middle-of-the-road one, from which few of us would diverge markedly—but I may be wrong there. Bob Solomon brought up a rather interesting international issue: the question of the extent to which one should try, by international action, to harmonize national behavior. I happen to take the opposite view from the one that I think is implicit in his analysis; I think that it is a rather lost cause to attempt to integrate national policies by international action.

There is another aspect of the international monetary problem that hasn't received a great deal of attention in the discussion thus far, and that is the problem of international liquidity. Do the conditions under which we now live make that problem less important than it was—I mean, do we have to worry about the international money supply in a floating world? If we do, then we have to turn to the question of how to solve the gold problem and how to solve the problem that we are still—more than ever—on a currency standard, on a currency-reserve system.

RONALD I. McKINNON: I'd like to bring up a topic which nobody has addressed directly, although Art Laffer alluded to it, and that is fiscal policy. In his opening remarks, Lord Robbins reached, I think, a broad consensus of agreement on monetary policy. His distinction between when monetary policy can be thought of as exogenous and when it is to be considered endogenous was very good, but there is no basic agreement in the profession at the present time, surprisingly enough, on fiscal policy. In particular, something Bob Solomon said made me a little worried—the notion that the major countries of the world should get together and agree on anti-recessionary policies, much like the Chancellor of the Exchequer, cited by Lord Robbins, going around, hat in hand, to various countries, trying to get them to expand. In this connection, what people appear to have in mind are very large fiscal deficits of the sort that Congress is currently contemplating.

There is an important analytical issue here—namely, is this really an anti-recessionary fiscal policy? Could, in fact, we be reducing output and employment by such large budget deficits in a time horizon somewhat longer than the three or six months that one might have in mind? In breaking down this subject, we might look at an open economy, such as Britain— one where the balance of payments is very dominant and where Keynesian fiscal policy in the form of very large deficits has been in effect for a considerable period. Such a policy involves the floating of a large amount of debt which passes out through the exchange markets and thereby raises the exchange rate relative to the domestic price level. One can make a case that this may reduce real output and employment in Britain. But even in a more closed economy like the United States, with the $70 billion or $80 billion deficit we are now contemplating, can we comfortably believe that the deficit is going to be expansionary in its effect on output and employment? I think this is a subject well worth exploring.

ROBERT W. OLIVER: I would like to add a footnote to some suggestions made already. In the process of evaluating the experience with a floating exchange-rate system, I hope we can ask Lord Robbins and perhaps others to say a word about how the world might get back to something that might be called a Bretton Woods type of system. It seems to me that the longer we have a floating-rate system, whether managed or dirty, the more difficult it is going to be to get back.

The next point I want to suggest for possible discussion has to do with the Fourth World—the question of development finance. This is a subject we have skirted several times in our various conferences. I think it was Fritz Machlup, at our conference two years ago, who said that the United States should have a current-account surplus large enough to finance not only private long-term capital outflow but also a very substantial level of aid. He contended that the U. S. balance of payments cannot be regarded as being in equilibrium unless this large current-account surplus exists.

But we have never gotten around to discussing figures. The so-called Second Development Decade began in 1970 with the suggestion that the wealthier nations should contribute something approaching 1 percent of their gross national product to development, yet the world has come nowhere near this goal. Indeed, development assistance as a percent of GNP has been declining in the present decade. Furthermore, the oil-price increases have created payments problems which have made the United States and other developed countries less anxious to participate in aid, whether bilateral or multilateral. It has been increasingly difficult, for example, for the World Bank to obtain the financing it has requested. Mr. McNamara now alleges that something like $36 billion of development assistance through IDA-type financing over a four-year period is needed simply to deal with the absorptive capacity that is now estimated to exist in the Fourth World. The question I would put is this: Is it possible for the OECD countries, let us say, not only to deal with their collective balance-of-payments problems but also to do so in such a way that assistance to the Fourth World is at the very least maintained—and preferably increased— through some sort of cooperative action?

ISAIAH FRANK: My suggestion follows from what Professor Oliver has just said and from Bob Solomon's suggestion that we talk a little more specifically about the implications of the oil-price increases. Bob mentioned the problem of allocating the current-account deficit among the oil-importing countries. I think there's a broader implication that perhaps we should address ourselves to relating to the Fourth World, and that is how the OPEC success in obtaining an additional $100 billion of resources per year has inspired the developing countries to seek similar arrangements for other commodities.

Of course, the OPEC transfer completely dwarfs any transfers in the form of foreign aid. I believe the developing countries now view commodity policy, and more specifically producer
cartels, as a kind of leading edge of what they call a new international economic order. A charter has been formally adopted
in the United Nations which lays out the specifics of what it is.
One element in it is the notion which Lord Robbins referred to
in his introductory remarks as indexation. He discussed the
matter in a domestic context, in the sense of tying wages and
other obligations to some sort of price index. The developing
countries have formally proposed indexation internationally, in
the sense of some sort of terms-of-trade protection. They feel
that the terms of trade should not be something that just happens; rather, they feel that, through commodity agreements
which intervene in the market and through buffer stocks on a
wide range of commodities, the terms of trade should be guar-
anteed and that the measures making this possible should be
approved of as a means of transferring resources to them.

In the past, when questions of this sort have arisen, the
United States officially has been inclined to dismiss such ideas
as making no economic sense and as of no importance. My
feeling is that now they can no longer be dismissed; they must
be addressed very specifically, and a very clear response must
be produced. Marina Whitman referred to supply factors as
having become more important. That, too, has an international
dimension. The international dimension is that, in our past
concerns about international trade, we have been overwhelm-
ingly preoccupied with the question of access to markets. We
have no international rules or principles that are worth anything relating to access to supplies, and this is one of the subjects in the multilateral trade negotiations. This is an area in
which the developing countries are very resistant to any formal
adoption of a set of rules, so I'm not sure that we know exactly
how to proceed. But I think there is little question of the great
importance of the whole subject of how one insures reasonable
access to supplies at a time when countries, for a variety of
reasons, are impeding that access—one of the reasons of course
being to contain domestic inflation.

H. C. McCLELLAN: The points I want to raise have been
mentioned, but I want to put a little inflection on each of them.
One of them has to do with the problem of dealing with the OPEC
countries. It seems to me that, as Lord Robbins pointed out
this morning, they may have overreached themselves. The

OPEC countries have real needs, however, and it seems to me that there might be developed a plan, a discussion of ideas, that could be used in negotiating amicable and satisfactory arrangements. A major question is what role industry should play in such a negotiation. The other matter I want to mention is the problem of capital formation. A few days ago, the president of Chase Manhattan Bank stated that, in his judgment and in the opinion of economists working at that bank, the world would face a major capital shortage within the next ten years. I would be interested in the views of other members on that subject.

SVEN W. ARNDT: Just a word on stagflation. One way in which to interpret the present stagflation is simply to recognize that we have excess demand and insufficient capacity in some sectors, whereas in other sectors we have excess supply; we are pushing against the capacity constraint in some areas, but have not reached it in others. In traditional models, the assumption of course would be that, except for short-term difficulties, there would be a flow of resources from the depressed areas into those where insufficient capacity was a problem. But, for all sorts of reasons, such a flow might be frustrated.

FRANK M. TAMAGNA: I agree with the point just made by Professor Arndt and, like Marina Whitman, I think we may be generalizing too much. For instance, the United States has 21 percent unemployment in one area and 3 percent in another. The same is true internationally, with some countries still enjoying high boom conditions while others clearly are not. Thus I think that in these discussions we should ask ourselves whether we can have generalized policies in a world in which depression and boom exist side by side.

Chairman THORP: I think enough has been said for me to announce a provisional agenda for our conference. It has interested me that the topic which has come up most often has been how floating exchanges are working and how, in the light of our experience with floating, we should deal with such questions as what to do about gold and how to handle SDRs. In other words, there has been much talk today about how the international monetary system now operates and how it may be threatened or inadequate. I would suggest, therefore, that we begin by trying to get a common feeling about how the system is working. After that, we can go on to the problems; and here I have the impression that Lord Robbins' general categories fit quite

well.   If we take the complicated presence of inflation and depression for one session, and the OPEC problems along with
the implicit broader supply problems for other commodities
for another session, we could conclude by considering some
broad general questions which I won't take the trouble to enu-
merate but which are all concerned with impending dangers
and how we rate these in order of importance.   With this kind
of rough outline, I am confident that each of you will be able to
get into the discussion the issues with which you are most concerned.

IV. STAGFLATION AND THE INTERNATIONAL MONETARY SYSTEM

Robert Triffin and
Conference Members

Chairman THORP: We now come to the first item on our agenda, which is a look at the present structure of the foreign-currency market—the dirty float, the managed float, and such matters. Because of his great knowledge of the subject, I have asked Robert Triffin to open the discussion, describing what the situation is now and indicating his assessment of what the problems are and what lines of action should be pursued. After his statement, we will have a general discussion of the topic.

ROBERT TRIFFIN: I would like to begin by paying a tribute to the opening remarks of Lord Robbins, with which I find myself in hearty agreement. I agree especially with his illuminating remark about politicians having eaten of the fruit of the Tree of Knowledge, because I think that, whether we like it or not, we cannot erase knowledge and we cannot prevent politicians from using the power which this knowledge has given them. I agree that we simultaneously face the problem of inflation—long-standing inflation, in fact—and of serious recession or depression. And I venture a new word for it; since I believe that this recession or depression stems from the inflation, I think we should reverse the usual order of words and call it "inflession"—inflation leading to recession.

I also agree with Lord Robbins that there are deep-root causes of the inflation that should be distinguished from the monetary permissiveness which has allowed it to develop the way it has. With respect to these root causes, however, I

would differ slightly from him. He stressed primarily the
wage push and the trade-union demands for higher wages. I
don't disagree with that, but I think the problem is broader,
and I would like to distinguish some other reasons for the inflation. The first is that we have lived for the last two hundred
years in what future historians may consider a very brief inter-
val in the history of the world—an era of enormous development
of material production and consumption beginning with the Industrial Revolution and continuing later with what I would call the
"Advertising Revolution, " which created new desires rather
than satisfying existing ones. This development has been aggra-
vated or accelerated by our postwar success, at least until recently, in fighting recessions. Another factor—and I would put
a great deal of stress on this point—has been the fantastic ex-
plosion of world military expenditure to $200 billion or $250 billion a year. This, to my mind, is the main cause of the inflation and of the U. S. payments deficit.

These real causes of inflation would not, of course, have
produced the kind of results in price and wage increases that
we see now if it had not been for the monetary permissiveness
which allowed rates of money creation far in excess of what
could be absorbed by the increase in production. This permissiveness occurred first on a national scale, but later extended to the international monetary system itself; I would like to
stress the fact that in the short space of three years—from the
end of 1969 to the end of 1972—international monetary reserves
doubled; in other words, as much reserves were created in
three years as had previously been created since Adam and
Eve. That was the outcome of an international monetary system which accepted a national currency, the U. S. dollar, as
an international asset.

And there is no limit, of course, to the expansion of the
system. If we look at the past five years (from the end of 1969
to the end of 1974), more than $100 billion—$101.7 billion, to be
exact—of the expansion of gross monetary reserves came from
the extension of credit by the international monetary system
itself, gold having played a totally insignificant role. Measured
in SDRs, the increase in gold reserves was only about $250 mil-
lion. And while we pay lip service to the principle that the rich
countries should export capital to the poor, in the one area
which theoretically is most completely under our control—international monetary credit—$100 billion of credit creation by the
international monetary system was for the benefit of the rich

countries (notably, of course, the United States), while the less
developed countries received only $3 billion. This impresses
me as highly ironic, particularly since, as we all remember,
the main objection of central bankers a few years ago to the
creation of SDRs was that it would encourage inflation by the
developing countries.

I will now touch briefly on the oil problem. It is surely sad
that the first response to the oil problem has been to put on ice
any thought of international monetary reform in the near future.
People are not ready to accept any commitments that they might
feel unable or unwilling to honor tomorrow, so reform is post-
poned as far as fundamental measures are concerned.   This
means that, even if the oil problem were solved immediately,
the major engine of world inflation would still be with us.

Let me say a word about flexible rates in relation to international monetary problems. Flexible rates have not provided
a solution. In the past year, the increase of world monetary
reserves has continued at an annual rate of about 20 percent—
far in excess of what could be absorbed by the increase in production. The system is managed or dirty or whatever you want
to call it, but let's use the term managed, as Professor Haberler has suggested; the point is that the system has been managed
in such a way as to continue to inflate the world monetary system.   The surpluses accumulated by the oil countries have not
been paid for by a reduction in reserves in other countries; they
have been paid for by the expansion of world reserves.

I agree with Professor Haberler and others that, in the circumstances into which we have let ourselves be pushed, flexible
rates may have become inevitable, and may be the lesser evil,
but I would like to stress that they are inevitable because of the
failure of our policies and of our international monetary system.
I don't see flexible rates as a goal or as a system but as a
second-best policy; and what I regret most of all, not only in
this connection but in many others, is that so many economists
have become advocates of the second-best. They apparently
think that people who ask for their counsel won't listen to their
first-best advice, so they rush to the second-best and thus per-
petuate the source of our troubles.

Chairman THORP: Are you going to tell us what the first-
best is?

TRIFFIN: If you wish, but I think I should do that in answer
to each individual problem as it is raised. On the matter of
flexible rates, I would answer that the first-best solution is

a reform of the international monetary system and, especially, of the existing highly inflationary mechanism of reserve crea- tion—a mechanism which has frustrated the process of inter- national adjustment and has involved massive lending by the poor countries to the rich.

Let me raise a point on the statement by Bob Solomon. He said that the main responsibility for anti-recessionary policies should fall on Germany, Japan, and the United States. He gave three reasons, the third of which was that these three countries had less serious balance-of-payments problems than other countries.

SOLOMON: They were said to.

TRIFFIN: They were said to. But in making such a judg- ment, one should bear in mind the remarks already made in this room about the weakness of the dollar. And one should also bear in mind Professor Oliver's point, with which I agree: that we in the United States must aim not simply at a balance on current account but, if we believe in what we say, at a large current-account surplus in order to help the developing nations.

In conclusion, it seems to me that there are two major top- ics that we should discuss. The first is international monetary reform, on which I have already given my views. The second is what I call "anti-inflession" policies. In regard to this sec- ond problem, the conservatives like to stress the need to return to free markets. This may be admirable in terms of expanding production, but it is not so admirable in the allocation of very scarce resources. We could not accept free markets in war- time, because the free-market answer to the allocation of scarce resources is to charge what the traffic will bear. This is not only inflationary but also unjust and humanly unacceptable, be- cause it perpetuates profligate ways while cutting down the satisfaction of essential needs. I hear that, in the automobile industry, the only cars that are doing well now are the Cadil- lacs; that's the free market's answer to the energy crisis.

At the other extreme, we have the interventionists, who count on government to solve all problems. When we ask econ- omists today about how to deal with the inflession problem, they generally rush to give the answer with which they are familiar; they know how to fight recession, but they have never had the problem of fighting recession and inflation at the same time, so they give advice about fighting recession with the old tools of aggregative macroeconomics: cutting taxes and increasing expenditure. And 80 percent of that may simply increase

inflation, with 20 percent trickling down to the alleviation of
unemployment and recession.   This is why I agree very much
with Marina Whitman that we have to develop as a first-best
solution appropriately selective microeconomic anti-inflession
policies.

RANDALL HINSHAW: Robert Triffin has stolen some of my
thunder, so I can be brief. Sir Roy Harrod remarked at one
of our conferences that over the years he had experienced much
mental turmoil over the issue of flexible exchange rates, sometimes being inclined to support them and sometimes being opposed. I did my graduate work at Princeton, where one could
hardly escape without being strongly in favor of flexible rates.
I supported them during the 1950s as an alternative to the exchange restrictions and currency inconvertibility which prevailed
during the early postwar years. But in the present setting of
world inflation, my attitude toward flexible rates is far from
enthusiastic, as I am persuaded that, globally speaking, they
have an inflationary bias —and a rather strong one. The problem is that, under floating, a country has no binding balance-
of-payments constraint on its domestic economic behavior, and
thus can be more relaxed in pursuing inflationary policies.

Our last conference was held right after the second dollar
devaluation of February 1973. I was very uneasy about that
development, as I was convinced that the decline of the dollar
was having a much bigger effect on the U. S. price level than
was the view of many economists —for example, Herbert Stein,
then Chairman of the Council of Economic Advisers, who, according to the Wall Street Journal, doubted that the second
devaluation would raise the U. S. cost of living by more than
one-tenth of 1 percent. That period was shortly followed by a
substantial further depreciation of the dollar which, combined
with the delayed effects of the two formal devaluations, was
directly responsible, in my opinion, for much of the double-digit
inflation that ensued.

My opinion was based on work I had done many years earlier
at the Federal Reserve Board on the 1933-34 devaluation of the
dollar. Franklin D. Roosevelt, as we all know, actually tried
to raise the U. S. commodity price level by raising the price
of gold. The reasoning was faulty, but the outcome was as
President Roosevelt had wished, because raising the dollar
price of gold had a profound effect on exchange rates; on a trade-
weighted basis, the dollar price of foreign currencies rose by
about 40 percent. One can show by figures and charts that there

was an amazingly high correlation during 1933 and 1934 between
the weighted dollar price of foreign currencies and the U. S.
wholesale price level, which in the last quarter of 1934 was 27
percent higher than in the first quarter of 1933. But the correlation is not hard to explain. For a rise in the dollar price of
foreign currencies raises not only the dollar price of imports
but also the dollar price of goods made from imports, the dollar price of goods competing with imports, and—via commodity
arbitrage—the dollar price of "exportables," part of which are
exported but much of which (beef and grain, for example) are
consumed domestically.

Gottfried Haberler raised the question of whether the dollar
is undervalued. This is not an easy question to answer. The
problem is that when the dollar goes down—and when the U. S.
price level consequently goes up—the upward movement of wages
and prices may induce a new round of inflationary policies aimed
at avoiding the unemployment that would otherwise occur. The
temptation to take inflationary action in these circumstances is
very strong, as the present Congressional mood illustrates.
But such action would, of course, create a new—and lower—
equilibrium position for the dollar in the exchange markets.
Thus the danger is that, as the dollar moves downward, it is
not necessarily moving below some stable equilibrium position
toward which it will tend to return but, instead, is inducing
policies which create successively lower equilibrium positions.

OLIVER: May I ask Randall to clarify what he means by
depreciation of the dollar creating its own new equilibrium.
Does he mean that prices go up accordingly?

HINSHAW: Prices go up; then, if there is accommodating
monetary and fiscal policy, as there well may be, there will
be a new equilibrium position which will be lower than the old
position, whatever that was. Adverse speculation can, of course,
cause the dollar to be undervalued, but this situation can itself
produce inflationary temptations which, if not resisted, can
quickly remove the undervaluation.

LAFFER: That's a nice place to come into the discussion—
right there. One of the major questions concerning a change
in exchange rates is the independence of the money supply.
Very few governments today can maintain a constant money
supply when prices rise because of the pressure to prevent a
fall in employment. So what we find is that, after a devaluation, countries tend to expand their money supplies, with little
if any tendency for countries with rising exchange rates to

reduce their money supplies. Thus I agree with Randall that flexible exchange rates tend to increase world inflation.

LEONARD S. SILK: On the question of the effect of floating, it seems to me very difficult to say whether the system is working very much better or very much worse than the preceding system, because of the general environment in which floating is taking place. Exchange rates broke down in a period of crisis. We had inflation before exchange rates broke down; we have even more inflation now. The causes are perhaps somewhat different. Before, world inflation was due mainly to dollar outflows; now, presumably, it is due mainly to a lack of discipline. Of course we had lack of discipline before the system collapsed, but everybody agrees that there is less discipline under floating rates.

The only respect in which, it seems to me, we can really argue that floating rates are an improvement is that we get fewer newspaper headlines about international monetary crises—crises of the pound, crises of the dollar, crises of the mark. Now that is not a minor difference; it is a very important difference. I think that the degree of stability under floating, such as it is, is in large measure due to the relative lack of hysteria in which the system accommodates itself to continuing problems. And we shouldn't despise it for that.

Chairman THORP: Are you saying that publicity concerning changes in exchange rates is less disturbing than publicity concerning declining reserves?

SILK: No, I mean that when a pegged rate is expected to be changed, large numbers of people—speculators and so forth—begin to rush out of one currency into another, and that is very disturbing to the system. I think that we get a somewhat smoother adjustment process under floating rates; floating is not as crisis-prone as, in the existing circumstances, a fixed-rate system would be.

The other point I want to make concerns the matter of what Bob Triffin likes to call "inflession" and what other people have called "inflump," "stagflation," "slumpflation," and so on. This is a somewhat new situation, and some of the reasons for it have been cited. I won't go through all of them, but they certainly do include that part of the fruit of the Tree of Knowledge which is attributed to Lord Keynes. It seems to me that the familiar Keynesian medicine—whether you call it Keynesian, Friedmanian, real cash-balance Friedmanian, or anything else—may be a very inappropriate way of dealing with present problems, because if we try to stop the inflation by cutting demand greatly, we aggravate a depression that the inflation has helped to cause; or if, on the other side, we try to treat the depression by simply pouring in more demand, we aggravate the inflation.

Now how can we deal with this problem? I am sure that Marina Whitman is right in saying that part of the answer is micro—that is, specific projects to deal with specific supply shortages. But I think that the specifics—especially when we're dealing with something as vast as energy—really add up to something more than can be described as micro. They move us toward a planning approach to life both domestically and internationally. In the old days, when people either out of innocence or out of weakness were willing to play a market game, we could have price determination in the way it was supposed to work according to textbook models. But when we get into situations of monopoly or of duopolistic warfare, then the old Walrasian models are not particularly helpful. And if the brave new world is going to consist of this kind of monopolistic warfare, much of which is political in origin, then, it seems to me, we are going to have to have new institutions to deal with the new problems. There are characteristics of this stagflation or whatever we want to call it that are really new, and I must say I get bored when I hear very old and familiar remedies prescribed for it.

Chairman THORP: Leonard has stirred up some reactions. Professor Sohmen has the floor.

EGON SOHMEN: As many of you know, I have for a long time endorsed flexible exchange rates. Let me begin by saying that I have not changed my mind. Many people have changed their minds on this question, but, where that has happened, the explanation, I think, is that they had expected something different from what they had reason to expect.

For example, on the inflation issue, it seems to me perfectly clear that liberation of the exchange markets from rigid pegging removes the lid from domestic inflation and that, if a country is embarked on an inflationary policy, the liberation of the exchanges will simply reinforce the inflation. But much of the inflation that we have had in the last few years has been a hangover from the Bretton Woods system and from the continuous pumping of more liquidity into the international monetary system before its final breakdown. We all know that inflation simply cannot be stopped abruptly once it has taken

hold—once expectations have adjusted to it.   In a country like
England, I would agree that removal of exchange-rate pegging
has added to domestic inflation.   But I think people should have
expected this; if they haven't, they simply have not thought
deeply enough about the matter.

What the removal of exchange-rate pegging does is to let
each country pursue its own counter-cyclical policy more or
less independently of the rest of the world.   If a country is
embarked on a very expansionary policy, then, of course, it
has more inflation if it lets the exchange rate float.   Under
floating, each country has greater freedom in dealing with its
domestic economic problems, and I think this is the way things
ought to be.   One of the distinct advantages of the system is
that it removes the need for the excessive international coordination and consultation that have been necessary from crisis to crisis in recent years.   I do not think that it is a sensible
system to have one country, say Western Germany, in any way
accountable for British monetary policy.   The British are a
grown-up people, and should be entitled to have their own monetary policy.   I would even say that England may need a taste
of the kind of inflation which Germany had in the 1920s in order
to convince the British government, the British trade unions,
and the British people that excessive monetary expansion is
not a workable policy.   Once this has happened, I am sure that
the British would be as well equipped as anybody to have a
different policy.

There are some people who say that we have no alternative
for the time being except flexible rates but that, once the crisis has passed, we should go back to something else.   Well, I
am not such an optimist as to believe that we won't have any
crises in the future, but, quite apart from this, it really puz-
zles me why some people think that a system which performs
better under crisis conditions would perform worse under more
normal conditions.   The subject would require some analysis
as to where the break-even point is—the point beyond which
one system becomes better than the other.   I haven't seen such
an analysis, but I think that what we would find under more normal conditions is simply that flexible rates would be more stable
than under crisis conditions.   Because we started from a rather
severe crisis, nobody should be surprised that the pendulum,
having been loosened, has swung sharply backwards and for-
wards.   Once the oil crisis is solved one way or another, the
major reason for large rate fluctuations will have disappeared,

so that exchange rates will probably be much more stable.

Let me turn to the so-called undervaluation of the dollar. I think this can be fairly easily explained by the fact that the United States in the last year or so has had a rather restrictive fiscal policy—not deliberately but simply as a result of the rising price level, which, under a progressive tax system, takes away more and more income from the public. One of the effects has been to bring down the interest rate, encouraging an outflow of capital and, as a result, a fall in the dollar on the exchange markets.

Chairman THORP: Mr. Sohmen, I can't let you speak any longer, because several people want to intervene; if you throw out any more of these sparks, we'll be burned up in no time. The next member on my list is Professor Scitovsky.

TIBOR SCITOVSKY: I would like to register agreement with Egon Sohmen on the proposition that when we move from fixed to flexible exchange rates, we have added an inflationary factor of major importance. It is one that Robert Triffin used to warn us about several years ago; he called it the "ratchet effect." I can't help feeling that this is quite important. Under fixed exchange rates, inflation was exported from deficit countries to surplus countries through an excess-demand effect. In addition to that kind of transmission, we now have another kind—namely, the rise in the prices of tradable goods in the countries with depreciating rates. This, I think, is really an important additional inflationary factor.

One more point. When Randall Hinshaw was talking about the movement of the equilibrium rate in response to the actual rate, it occurred to me that this may be an explanation for the disappointment of our hopes that futures markets would be available to provide adequate insurance and stability under a flexible exchange-rate system. Those futures markets have failed to develop, and one reason may be that there is no objective basis on which to judge the future long-run equilibrium rate: the long-run rate simply drifts in the direction it is already moving.

TRIFFIN: My remarks are brief, because I agree with what Tibor said. Historically, I think that everyone will have to agree that we would not have moved from adjustable fixed rates to flexible rates if it had not been for the doubling of world monetary reserves that confronted Germany with an incredible flood of dollars to absorb. Moreover, I would stress what Tinbergen has said many times—that there is a limited degree

of tolerance for any single weapon of policy. For instance, in
the last three months, the German mark has gone up more than
15 percent in terms of the dollar. There is a limit to what
German industry can accept in this respect because of the effect on export competition. I would stress that flexible rates
are not a panacea; they are not a substitute for reforming the
adjustment mechanism and the system of international monetary reserve creation. If the United States, like other countries, had been forced to finance its payments deficits out of
its own reserve assets, it would not have been able to sustain
reserve losses of nearly $100 billion since World War II.

SOHMEN: It would have floated sooner.

TRIFFIN: But it would not have created world inflation.

Chairman THORP: Your minute is a bit inflated. Mr.
Jamison:

CONRAD C. JAMISON: Dr. Sohmen, you used the term
"flexible exchange rates," and that covers a lot of territory.
I was wondering if you were thinking specifically in terms of
the "crawling peg."

SOHMEN: No, I was referring rather vaguely to what we
now have, which is not the extreme form of flexibility without
intervention, as we all know, but what some people call dirty
floating or managed floating. I was not thinking of a crawling
peg with narrow limits such as you may have in mind.

Chairman THORP: In other words, flexible but managed
and without established limits.

SOHMEN: Yes.

ALIBER: I have a question for Egon. When I listen to him,
I don't know whether I am getting a chapter out of a textbook
or a description of recent history; I hope it's the second, but
it sounds like the first. Since March 1973, we have had two
periods of rather sharp movement in exchange rates: the first
was in the spring of 1973 and the other has been during the past
four months. Are both of these to be interpreted as hangovers
from the Bretton Woods system? Or do they both reflect the
normal operation of independent monetary policies under a
floating exchange-rate regime?

SOHMEN: I think I have already answered these questions.
As far as the fall of 1973 is concerned, everybody knows that
this is when the oil crisis occurred.

ALIBER: The sharp appreciation of foreign currencies in
terms of the dollar occurred in the spring of 1973—not in
the fall.

SOHMEN: Well, as I said before, when you hold the pendulum too far out of equilibrium, you would expect the swings to be rather large. I wouldn't blame anybody in the market for misjudging the future movement of exchange rates in such a situation. As for the depreciation of the dollar in the last six months, I think that the level now is fairly close to what one should expect. The dollar may have gone a bit too far down, but I really do not believe that it is excessively far out of line with the equilibrium rate under present conditions.

WALTER S. SALANT: With respect to the fall of the dollar in 1973, I don't think that Egon's pendulum analogy will work. The float commenced in March, and for two months there was no excessive reaction. The dollar remained quite stable; it was not until May that it began to go down continuously and rapidly through July. So I think we need to look for another reason. More generally, it seems to me that, just as in the stock market, we get quite exaggerated movements. I don't see why the foreign-exchange market should behave any differently from the stock market; the only difference is that the foreign-exchange market is far more important.

STEVEN W. KOHLHAGEN: I want to speak in support of Egon, who really needs some support at this moment. If we were to characterize the foreign-exchange market of the last two years, I think we would have to describe it as clearly being over-reactive to news, speculative forces, economic events, and information. In his statement a few minutes ago, Professor Scitovsky referred to the inadequate development of a forward market as a source of weakness in the current floating regime. In this regard, there may be a parallel with the U. S. domestic money market in the 1950s. I have heard the theory that, until short-term interest rates rose in the mid-1950s, commercial banks could not justify the cost of the personnel needed for the development of programs to manage their asset portfolios. One can use the same argument with respect to forward markets. Until exchange rates began fluctuating significantly a year or two ago, corporations and banks were not in a position to justify training the personnel for dealing with these markets. The implication is that, just as it took banks five or six years to perfect the management side of their domestic asset portfolios, it may well take banks a similar period to develop the management of their foreign-exchange assets and liabilities. I don't think that the last two years offer a fair test for a flexible-rate regime in view of the severe external shocks the system has been facing.

McKINNON: My point is related to the point just made —
about whether there is learning by doing in the foreign-exchange
market. One might well think that, broadly speaking, a bank
would look at management of its foreign-exchange position in
much the same way as it looks at management of its domestic
asset portfolios. But I think that what we observe in practice
is negative learning by doing, because the foreign-exchange
market is primarily an interbank market which is closed to all
but the fifty best-known names in the banking business. Because
of the various bankruptcies that we have observed and because
of large foreign-exchange losses of several leading banks, all
banks have directives to be very conservative in managing their
foreign-exchange positions. Not only do they have to have balanced positions in any one currency, but they now have to have
balanced positions at every maturity in any given foreign currency. So the most natural institutions for speculating in the
foreign exchanges — indeed, the only ones that have ready access
to daily speculation — are excluding themselves; and if they don't
exclude themselves, then their central banks, quite correctly,
will exclude them from taking risks of this kind. Thus there
are serious institutional barriers against having Friedman-like
speculators entering the market and taking obvious positions
that can be held for a period of three to six months.

Chairman THORP: I think this bears on something Professor De Cecco wants to bring in.

MARCELLO DE CECCO: Yes; what I have to say is very
short. I would say that, to break even in the forward exchange
market, you need to have a roulette wheel without the zero.
As played thus far, it has been roulette with a zero, and banks
don't like to act as casino operators with this sort of game. In
fact, no casino operator likes that.

TAMAGNA: I would like to say a word or two about the factors which have influenced the dollar exchange rate in the past
year. The dollar depreciated in the first and last quarters of
1974, and appreciated in the second and third. In explaining
these developments, two factors seem to me important. In
the first place, U. S. monetary policy was easy in the first
and last quarters and tight in the second and third quarters —
particularly the third. Thus the capital movement into the
United States was highest in the second and third quarters. In
the last quarter, U. S. loans abroad went up, because interest
rates went down sharply in New York but didn't go down abroad.

In the second place, there has been an increasing tendency on the part of the Arab countries that have invested heavily in the United States to diversify their oil earnings—partly by direct investment in Europe.

TRIFFIN: Let me add a longer-term observation to what Frank has just said. In Europe, many have been predicting a strong dollar, because the United States is less vulnerable than Europe in regard to oil. I have made the opposite prediction that it will be a weak dollar. My reason is that, for the oil-exporting countries, the dollar is still the instrument through which payments are made. Whether we are in deficit or the Italians are in deficit or Bangladesh is in deficit, it is dollars that go to the Arabs. For the dollar not to weaken, the Arabs would have to spend or invest in the United States all the dollars they receive from the rest of the world, and I doubt very much that they will do this. They will be increasing their imports much more rapidly than expected; these imports are traditionally one-half to two-thirds from Western Europe and only about 10 percent from the United States. Of course, the Arabs will take any military equipment that we are willing to sell them, but they will not want to depend entirely on the United States as a source in the case of a war with Israel; they will want to diversify, obtaining some of their weaponry from Western Europe. So far as investments are concerned, the Arab countries are worried about the possible blocking of their accounts by the U. S. Treasury. Thus they have an additional inducement to invest in Europe rather than in the United States. Finally, there is the fact that whereas four or five years ago companies engaging in international business kept all their working balances in dollars, they now want to diversify these balances. These considerations all point toward a weak rather than a strong dollar, and I therefore do not share the optimism of some of my European friends.

SOLOMON: I have a comment on Bob Triffin's argument. He says that the dollar is weak because people use the dollar as payment for oil. He implies that there is somehow an excess supply of dollars, but what he seems to have ignored is that, if the dollar is used as a currency of payment for oil, this means that Germans and Frenchmen and Swedes and Japanese have to buy dollars with their currencies in order to make such payments. There is a demand for the dollar in the foreign-exchange market as well as a supply, and Bob has looked at just one side.

My second point is also about the alleged weakness of the dollar. The big depreciation of the dollar occurred between June 1970, when the Canadian dollar was floated, and March 1973, when general floating began; according to Morgan Guaranty calculations, the U. S. dollar in March 1973 was 17.5 percent below its June 1970 level. Since March 1973, the net movement has been small; dollar depreciation in mid-February 1975 had increased only to 18.3 percent. So we've had only a miniscule net depreciation of the dollar since general floating began. Of course, there have been sizable movements in the dollar since floating which have been of considerable concern, but that is a different question from a secular weakness of the dollar—a weakness which I don't see in the figures.

THOMAS D. WILLETT: I would like to make a comment or two on the interpretations that are being given to the movements in the dollar. My first point is in regard to the relation between interest-rate movements and the rise and fall of the dollar. My staff at Treasury, some of the staff at Federal Reserve, and a number of private academic investigators have been doing some econometric work on this matter. The initial results of these studies appear to show that neither for the United States nor for the other major industrial countries is there a strong systematic relationship between interest-rate changes and exchange-rate changes during the current float. This I find rather surprising; I offer it as a reason for doubt rather than as definitive evidence either way.

On another matter, it is sometimes stated that the behavior of the dollar has been very erratic and that the foreign-exchange market has been thin. This carries the implication that systematic intervention might have stabilized the dollar and that systematic profits might have been forthcoming by following simple empirically derived rules of intervention. That matter has also been studied. The preliminary results I have seen point to the conclusion that it is not easy to define simple rules that would have made systematic profits.

SVEN GRASSMAN: I would like to raise the question of what we mean by an excessive movement in the exchange rate. Several members here today have stated or implied that there have been excessive exchange-rate movements, particularly in the dollar rate. This is by no means obvious to me. One of the virtues of the flexible exchange-rate system is that exchange rates actually can move. There may be erratic movements, but there are also equilibrating movements.

In the search for criteria in this connection, I think we have to look at the effect on international trade. There is no evidence that international trade has been harmed by the floating system. During 1973, we had the quickest expansion in international trade in history, both in nominal and in real terms. This mainly reflected, I think, the big expansion in income and activity all over the world, just as the slow development in 1974 reflected a slackening in economic activity in most countries.

Thus there is no evidence I know of that world trade has been harmed by the movement in exchange rates or by the floating system. Reinforcing this conclusion is the fact that forward transactions have not expanded very much. It has been implied here several times that the market has somehow failed to expand, but I am not sure that there has been a very big demand for forward cover. Traders perhaps did not suffer as much as generally thought by the swings in exchange rates, so there was not much increased demand for making use of the forward market.

KOHLHAGEN: Sven, you and I may have different data, but the people I've talked to have said that the forward market in the United States is down about 60 percent from what it was two years ago.

GRASSMAN: The situation is different in different countries. In Sweden, for instance, covered import and export transactions almost doubled from the middle of 1973 to the middle of 1974, but this doubling was from a very low level. I have noticed the decline in the United States, and I don't know the reasons.

WHITMAN: My reaction to the discussion of the past half hour is that there appears to be a convergence of views with respect to what floating rates do and don't do—not a total convergence, by any means, but a considerable degree of agreement. On the plus side, I think it is clear that floating rates haven't hurt world trade and world investment, as many people feared they would. International trade has been expanding, and while it may now be contracting because world production is contracting, the established relationships between output and trade appear to have been maintained; these relationships do not seem to have changed as a result of a change in the system. I think that it is also true that some of the fears associated with elasticity pessimism have been dispelled. Although the evidence is somewhat mixed, it seems clear that in the case of the United States, for example, dollar depreciation has improved the trade balance and the current-account balance, indicating that extreme elasticity pessimism was not justified.

TRIFFIN: The situation has been different in Germany.

WHITMAN: I know; as I said, the situation is mixed, and we have to look at other things too, including differences in macroeconomic policies. On the minus side, there have been some disappointing aspects of floating rates. For one thing, the floating regime has certainly not been accompanied by any great dismantling of controls on international transactions. This is perhaps putting it mildly; if anything, there has been a proliferation of controls, at least on capital account. Until now, countries have been rather good about not establishing beggar-my-neighbor policies on trade account, but certainly, with the exception of the United States, there has not been the general abolition of controls which many advocates of floating had expected.

Also on the minus side is some evidence of excessive exchange-rate movements as well as some evidence of, at the very least, a thinness in the kind of stabilizing speculation one would hope for. There are all kinds of theories as to why this has been so. In any case, we all probably have a bit more concern than before about the loss of efficiency in the use of money. When all is said and done, there are certain advantages in having an international money, and the change in the exchange-rate system has to some extent reduced the effectiveness of the dollar or anything else as an international money.

There is probably some loss here. If we look at private transactions, it is hard to see why the optimum currency area is not the world. For private transactions, there are many advantages in having a single money. The reason the optimum currency area may be smaller than the world is, I think, the demand of countries for separate national policies. And we need a system which reflects that fact. I conclude that if we have to keep a score card for floating rates, it would be a mixed one.

LAFFER: I would like to register a slight disagreement on the obviousness of the alleged favorable effect of dollar depreciation on the U.S. trade balance. I think it is by no means clear that depreciation improved the trade balance or the current-account position. The next thing I would say is that it is not at all obvious to me that the appropriate measure of welfare in the world economy is the volume of international trade. By means of subsidies and other measures, we could have a very high volume of world trade without any close correspon-

dence to comparative advantage, and this situation would clearly
be worse than less trade. Finally, I would like to understand
what has happened in Germany; the mark has appreciated, the
Germans import large amounts of oil, and yet the German trade
surplus is the highest ever.

SOLOMON: Art Laffer did not give evidence for the alleged
failure of dollar depreciation to improve the U. S. trade balance; he simply made an assertion. I would like to make a
counter-assertion that, in the case of both the United Kingdom
and the United States, the effect on the current account, if one
studies it, is quite visible and quite favorable.

Chairman THORP: I will apoint the two of you as a subcom-
mittee to go off wherever you want to in order to examine the
record. If you want to report back to us, you may; if you don't
want to, you don't need to. Wilson Schmidt:

WILSON E. SCHMIDT: Just a comment on whether dollar
movements have been excessive. Under the Smithsonian
arrangements of December 1971, members of the International
Monetary Fund agreed to set limits on exchange-rate variations which would permit up to a 9 percent shift of the exchange
rate between two countries. Looking at the high and the low
for the dollar in terms of the level in March 1973, it turns out
that the dollar changed, at most, by 10 percent. So we were
almost within those rules.

SILK: I have a question for Professor Sohmen. He said
that the unintended fiscal tightening in the United States accounts
for the weakening of the dollar. This sounds exactly counter
to the accepted wisdom of the past. I have always understood
that a tighter fiscal policy would tend to raise the exchange
rate, not to lower it. Did you mean what you said and, if so,
why?

SOHMEN: We have to differentiate between monetary policy
and fiscal policy. As concerns monetary policy, you are perfectly right; when a country has an expansionary monetary
policy, its currency depreciates. With fiscal policy, the story
is not so simple; the exchange rate can go either way, depending
among other things on the marginal propensity to import and—
which is very important—on how capital movements react to
changes in interest rates. A tight fiscal policy tends to reduce
imports, but it also tends to lower interest rates because of
reduced government borrowing. The decline of interest rates
may have an adverse effect on the international capital account,
thereby offsetting, or even outweighing, the favorable effect

on the balance of payments of the decline in imports. So the
exchange rate can move in either direction as a result of a
tighter fiscal policy; in the case of the United States, as I have
indicated, one can make a reasonable guess that a tight fiscal
policy encouraged a depreciation of the dollar.

Let me turn briefly to another matter. We have always been
told by private bankers that of course no bank, at least no responsible bank, ever speculates in the foreign-exchange market.
But we've seen that some banks really have speculated on a
large scale. Well, they probably overdid it in certain cases,
and now they are frightened and have largely withdrawn from
the market. I would guess that in the future banks probably
will again provide some welcome speculation of a stabilizing
character, though they may not do so on as large a scale as
some have in the recent past.

I think some movements in exchange rates can be explained
by the rather sudden changes in bank policies. For example,
after the move to flexible rates in March 1973, many banks
appear to have intervened rather heavily in a speculative way
in the exchange markets, and this may be one reason why for
a few weeks the dollar remained rather stable. Then, when
the banks decided that they had overestimated the strength of
the dollar, they apparently withdrew from the market, thus
accounting for at least part of the decline of the dollar at
that time.

Chairman THORP: Marcus Fleming wants to get into this
discussion.

FLEMING: My remarks are going to be about floating rates
too. Some of you may be a little tired of the subject by this
time, but I'll try to be as brief as possible.

Like Professor Hinshaw, I have been a floater; I've always
favored floating rates. I have moved a little bit in the direction of the center, perhaps, as a result of recent experience,
but not as far as he has. One thing that has tended to move me
against floating rates is the praise they have received from
some Johnnys-come-lately into this field, whose enthusiasm
for floating seems to derive largely from the fact that we no
longer have these disturbing crises in the newspaper headlines.
Except for giving ulcers to central bankers and Treasury officials, however, these crises, as far as I can see, never did
anybody any harm; and, important as it is not to give central
bankers ulcers, I don't think we should place that at the top
of our scale of priorities.

Whatever the merits on either side, it seems to me impossible to imagine doing without floating rates so long as we have these very large potential movements of capital. No other method of successfully controlling them has been devised. Direct capital controls obviously don't work. At the same time, countries are not willing to gear their monetary policies exclusively to the aim of stabilizing exchange rates. And if they are not willing to do that, I can't see much hope of keeping balance-of-payments fluctuations within bounds other than by letting the rates vary.

But the transition from pegging to intervening as a method of controlling exchange rates is all that may be involved in going over to flexible rates. It's simply a change, so to speak, from bank-rate policy to open-market policy. Viewed in that light, it seems to me that we can retain many of the basic objectives of the old Bretton Woods system, including exchange-rate stability, though defined in a slightly different way.

The experience since the oil-price increase seems to me to be the biggest argument for floating rates and for their inevitability under present conditions. The almost miraculous way in which we have gone through that period, with so little disturbance and with reserves of almost every important group of countries maintained fairly constant, is unimaginable under the par-value system as we knew it or under any system other than floating rates.

Having said that, however, I don't agree with those people who are satisfied with the degree of fluctuation which has prevailed generally under the floating system. I feel the fluctuations have been too big. These variations are not greatest for the dollar, because many countries peg loosely, or not so loosely, to the dollar. But if we look at the exchange rates of countries like Switzerland, Austria, Germany, Holland, Belgium, and France, we see bigger fluctuations. It may be true that these swings don't greatly exceed 10 percent, but even a 10 percent swing vis-a-vis the average of other rates seems unduly high. If I may say so, Professor Schmidt gave a misleading impression in implying that the 10 percent swing in the dollar was only a little greater than would have been allowed under the Smithsonian agreement, which envisioned that the rates between any two currencies might vary by as much as 9 percent. There is a big difference between setting a limit on the extent to which one country's currency can vary against each other currency and the extent to which it can vary against the average of all other currencies. Exchange rates have swung much more than they would have been allowed to under the par-value system—even as modified by the Smithsonian reform.

One's feeling that exchange rates may have swung too much is intensified by evidence that these swings have an asymmetrical effect on prices. They push prices up in the depreciating countries, and they don't pull prices down in the appreciating countries to the same extent; in other words, they exercise a net inflationary effect. As Marina Whitman pointed out, the old theory that floating rates would contain inflationary or deflationary forces within countries, and would thus lead to a desynchronization of cyclical movements, has not been borne out.

I think there are reasons for that. I don't want to embark on a long discussion, but if floating does not prevent the spread of cyclical movements and unemployment and if, as appears evident, it does have a bad influence on the trade-off between price movements and unemployment, thus intensifying the problem of stagflation, I think we have a pretty serious case against floating that has to be carefully weighed. It seems to me that what we ought to be thinking about is what can be done internationally to reduce the swings and to bring a measure of stability into the floating-rate system. What I would like to see is some system under which countries whose rates have wandered too far away from a reasonable estimate of medium-term equilibrium would be under an obligation to prevent further deviation and even to move back toward the norm not only by means of intervention but also by means of monetary policy.

I'm not suggesting that monetary policy be directed exclusively to external objectives; countries clearly are not willing to do that. But countries surely might do more than they have done in the past to take account of external objectives in pursuing their monetary policies, including their interest-rate policies. For this kind of system to succeed, countries have to be willing to discuss their rates of exchange and the range within which their rates ought, if possible, to be contained; they must stop regarding the exchange rate as such a frightful secret that nobody dare mention it explicitly, even within the walls of international institutions.

HABERLER: I want to go back for a moment to some basic questions raised by Lord Robbins and Robert Triffin. I fully agree with both of them that floating is a second-best approach.

The best arrangement is one which would copy what we have between the states in the United States—namely, absolutely fixed rates with no margins. That would be the ideal international system. But unfortunately we cannot have that. Such a system would mean that some countries would have much more inflation than they want, others would have unemployment, and many would introduce controls. Coordinating international economic policies—monetary policies, fiscal policies, and, some would add, incomes policies—is an exceedingly difficult matter. We see that in the Common Market. Here we have countries which cooperate very closely and discuss these things continuously, but still are not able to coordinate their policies sufficiently.

Of course, there are many cases in which some coordination is possible. There are about two dozen countries which peg to the dollar, including Mexico and several other Latin American countries. If they don't mind the inflation which they get from the United States, the arrangement is fine. If they get 10 percent inflation, that doesn't count; in Latin America, any price rise under 10 percent is deflation anyway. But if we take the European countries and Japan, they simply don't want to do that. Thus we are stuck with some sort of floating system.

The real question for the time being—and, I'm afraid, for a long time to come—is what kind of floating we want: clean, dirty, or managed. As I said earlier, I think we should make a distinction between managed floating and dirty floating—if by managed floating we merely mean official buying and selling in the exchange market in order to iron out short-run fluctuations or, if we want to go a little further, in order to influence medium-term trends. I think this is acceptable. But if we go beyond that; if we do what the Italians did with import restrictions, split markets, and multiple exchange rates, then managed floating becomes dirty floating, and that should be avoided as much as possible. I think this is really the problem.

And now in the recession, of course, protectionist temptations are tremendous. If we have a great deal of unemployment, it is very tempting to manipulate the exchange rate to get temporary relief. This has not yet been done on a large scale, and I hope things will stay that way. I hope that the International Monetary Fund will in the future give more attention to this problem, rather than worrying about how stable or adjustable exchange rates can be resurrected.

Just one more word. I read with much interest a recent
paper by Charlie Kindleberger. Charlie is perhaps the strong-
est advocate there is for fixed exchange rates and world money,
and in his paper he repeats all the familiar arguments for his
position. But he concludes that, although fixed rates are the
ideal, we just can't have them in the foreseeable future. When
Charlie says that, I find it very persuasive. Art Laffer, I think,
has not yet been persuaded.

TRIFFIN: I am delighted to be fairly close to Gottfried in
the remarks he has just made. He says that a fixed exchange-
rate system is the best one to aim at but that, unfortunately, we
cannot succeed in this aim. But I would not just go then to the
opposite extreme and say, let's have floating rates. I would
say, let's do as much as we can in the direction of the first-
best system. I would add that, in order to make any system
workable, the first thing we have to do is to eliminate the possibility of a flooding of international monetary reserves by a
so-called reserve currency. Before the dollar flood occurred,
the system of fixed but adjustable rates worked for many years
with reasonable success. Why do we give it up? Because we
refuse to face what the Group of Twenty has repeatedly affirmed—
that reserves in the future should be accumulated primarily in
the form of SDRs and that national currencies as reserves should
be phased out. We have read this I don't know how many times.
Dr. Emminger has said so again, adding that the task is difficult. But because it's difficult, we should not simply give up.

HABERLER: By all means, let's work for the ideal—that
is, coordinate national policies as much as possible. If we are
successful in that, the flexible rates will stabilize, and then, in
I don't know how many years, we shall be at the point where
major currencies can return to a fixed-rate system. But I think
it will take a very long time. In the meantime, I'm afraid, the
adjustable-peg system is inferior to the flexible-rate system.

Chairman THORP: I might explain that the reason Randall
Hinshaw has invited several very young people to this conference is that we hope that at least someone who is here will live
to see that remote day. One possibility is Tom Willett.

WILLETT: In discussing whether fixed rates are a first-
best approach, we need further clarification about what we mean
by first-best and about whether we're talking about political
constraints or economic constraints. For instance, I wasn't
fully clear whether Gottfried was referring to political realities
or economic realities. It seems to me that for the world to be

an optimum currency area, the requirements would include a high degree of mobility of the factors of production. In the absence of high factor mobility, it is not clear to me that a world currency is a first-best solution even if we have all the political will in the world for coordination. I entirely agree with Bob Triffin that economists should be very wary of making second-best recommendations where they are defining second-best as what they think is politically expedient. But the arguments for floating rates are by no means all in that category. My own view, apart from any political consideration, is that the world—on the basis of economic criteria alone—is not an optimum currency area.

To get back to a discussion we had earlier, a number of comments were made to the effect that floating rates have an adverse effect on inflation. I would like to take issue with that general conclusion. I don't think that the economics profession has arrived at a state of knowledge from which we can draw unambiguous conclusions about the comparative inflationary effects of alternative exchange-rate systems. If we are talking about a floating-rate regime, we have to decide what alternatives we are comparing it with. For instance, it is clear from Bob Triffin's comments that he would draw a distinction between the adjustable-peg system which led to the huge flooding of dollars into the rest of the world and his own preferred solution. Thus we might very well find out that, on inflation grounds, we would rate Bob's proposed system as first-best, floating rates as second-best, and the system replaced by floating as third-best.

In his remarks on floating rates, Tibor Scitovsky referred to the so-called "ratchet effect." I haven't seen a great deal of persuasive empirical evidence that this is a significant phenomenon, but it is certainly a factor which could worsen the inflation-unemployment trade-off. But consider the case of Germany, where the rate of domestic inflation is lower than the rate of world inflation. If Germany were to maintain a fixed exchange rate, the rest of the world would be imposing on it a progressively worse Phillips Curve—a progressively worse inflation-unemployment trade-off. If world inflation is 10 percent and German inflation is 5 percent, the only effective exchange-rate policy is to permit the mark to appreciate 5 percent a year.

One can argue that fixed exchange rates tend, on balance, to be inflationary, because under that system we get massive monetary flows requiring the surplus countries to inflate much more than the deficit countries are forced to deflate. But my general

feeling is that this is really an exceedingly complicated subject
on which it is premature to arrive at definitive conclusions.

Lord ROBBINS: I would like to interpose a distinction which
I think is implicit in what has just been said. It seems to me
that one could make a clear distinction between two fundamental
questions. The first is: does the possibility of floating in certain circumstances breed irresponsibility of domestic policy?
The second is: does the fact of exchange-rate movement give
rise to internal repercussions which are inflationary? I think
it is very important to keep these two questions absolutely
separate.

DE CECCO: I want to say to Tom Willett that when he cites
the German example, he shouldn't leave out of the picture a
rather interesting part of the adjustment mechanism—namely,
three million foreign workers. This is a rather important form
of adjustment discipline, I would say, and a matter often neglected by economists.

ALIBER: It may help us in our discussion of floating to take
a brief tour through history. During the twentieth century, we've
had three periods of floating rates: the 1920s, the 1930s, and the
period since early 1973. There is, I think, one thing in common
in each of these periods—namely, great uncertainty about price
levels and employment. In each of these periods, the failure
of domestic policies forced a move to floating rates because no
other system was feasible. And, in part, that is a way of saying that central bankers had lost their credibility. They had
been saying that pegged rates would work, that they would hold
on to their parities, and then they would renege on their commitments.

The central question that we have to ask at this time has to
do with the relationship between getting greater stability and
order into the international monetary system and getting greater
stability and order into domestic economies. If we try to impose greater stability and order in the exchange market without
taking care of what is happening in domestic economies, we will
simply give international negotiations another black mark. If
we get domestic stability, we will find that stability in the international monetary system will follow almost automatically.

HABERLER: Did I hear right about a floating system in
the 1930s?

ALIBER: Yes.

HABERLER: Then I must say that I find this a complete
misunderstanding. We had rigid trade controls in the 1930s,

but very little floating.

ALIBER: We had a floating rate for sterling.

HABERLER: Yes, but there was no general floating. In most cases, currencies were pegged either to sterling, the dollar, or gold. And the sterling float was, of course, a highly managed one.

SCITOVSKY: I would like to come back to our discussion about the inflationary effects of fixed versus flexible exchange rates. Tom Willett may be right that we don't yet have enough empirical evidence to reach firm conclusions at this stage, but I would still like to submit that there is a qualitative difference between the two systems in their inflationary impact. One familiar source of inflation, of course, is excess demand. But there is a very different kind of inflationary effect which has nothing to do with excess demand. An obvious example is the raising of the price of oil. This steep price increase was clearly inflationary, but it had nothing to do with excess demand. And under flexible exchange rates, there is likewise an inflationary impact on a depreciating country which has nothing to do with excess demand—which has to do solely with the rise in the prices of tradable goods, inducing a sort of cost-push sequence which is entirely separate and apart from any excess demand that might also be inflationary.

Chairman THORP: Earlier, I spoke about the young people we have here, so now I'll call on the Young brothers—first Arthur and then John.

ARTHUR N. YOUNG: There is a practical ground for worry which I hope will not prove serious but which I think ought to be recognized. We've talked about central bank intervention and dirty floating. There are cases in which knowledge of central bank objectives has become privy to people who are not as responsible as the central bankers, who by and large, I think, are very dependable individuals. For those in the know, this knowledge of objectives and of the levels of exchange rates that are intended could go beyond speculation: it's a sure thing which could have serious repercussions on the exchange market.

JOHN PARKE YOUNG: There are so many angles to our international monetary problems that it is hard to know just where to begin. I think a basic problem is the inability of the fluctuating dollar to serve satisfactorily as the international monetary standard. This has been made abundantly clear by recent events. The OPEC countries are turning to the SDR or some combination of currencies as a unit of account in place of the dollar. Some of the airlines are toying with the idea of using a composite unit; they are not waiting for the IMF to act.

The need, however, is broader than a stable unit for calculating transactions, important as that is. The OPEC countries as well as other countries are concentrating funds in a few of the stronger currencies, rather than being guided by broader economic considerations in the distribution of their liquid assets. The result is increasing imbalance and aggravation of the adjustment problem. It would be better if these funds were spread about more widely, including investment in the less developed countries, but monetary uncertainties impede such economic distribution not only of petrodollars but of other funds as well.

It is not necessary to belabor the inadequacies of the dollar standard or the difficulties it causes for international trade — the favor it bestows on the United States in permitting that country to pay for imports by pouring dollars on the world market, the contribution to world inflation from the large amount of dollars added to world reserves, and the absence of international control of world liquidity largely fed by these dollars. Monetary reform should be hastened, and should raise its sights by providing a stable medium of exchange for all international transactions.

At these meetings here and in Bologna, I have urged that the SDR be developed into an international currency—that is, that it be available to the private sector as well as to central banks for international transactions. I have noted that this could be done by authorizing the International Monetary Fund to open transferable deposit accounts with members in terms of the SDR. Central banks could make the SDR available to commercial banks in exchange for local currency, and commercial banks could make the SDR available to the public for international transactions. Such an IMF currency would make its way into use on a voluntary basis as determined by demand.

We are moving slowly and timidly toward an SDR standard. It has been agreed that the SDR shall become the principal reserve asset for central banks, but that is not enough. Private international transactions still have to worry along with fluctuating dollars. Capital still needs to move around in search of safety, thereby adding to instability. If the SDR is to meet today's needs, it must be available to the private sector. Unfortunately, modifications of the SDR now contemplated will not enable it to serve as a medium of exchange or to take the place of the dollar for international transactions. The SDR in its present form is essentially an interest-bearing note rather than a medium of exchange. If it were issued by the IMF as a simple transferable currency, it would not need to bear interest; it could earn interest by being invested in the market, and would be much more useful to central banks.

Of course there are political obstacles. As Jeremy Morse of the Committee of Twenty has said, "There is a lack of political will and cooperation, but no lack of competence." But public readiness to accept the SDR, as shown by recent events, is far ahead of political thinking. Thus international monetary reform should be both hastened and broadened.

McKINNON: John Young's discussion of the SDR is related quite closely to the point that I want to make. As I see matters, it is not so much that we need an international currency among central banks or among banks per se, but that we need a currency that is stable. It is not enough to issue the SDR; we must have some mechanism by which its real value in terms of goods and services is maintained. As far as I know, no convincing mechanism of this kind has been suggested for governing the issue of SDRs. Indeed, there are many claimants for the seignorage to be obtained from the issue of SDRs, and the more claimants there are, of course, the more difficult it is to stabilize the SDR's value.

I think this need for a riskless asset in the international monetary system in part explains why the current system of floating exchange rates is so unstable—surprisingly unstable, given the past literature on the subject and our experience with isolated examples of floating. The absence of private stabilizing speculators can, I think, be linked quite closely to the fact that there is no longer a single riskless asset in the system. This means that private speculation cannot be decentralized across national currencies.

If, for example, one makes the judgment that the Italian lira is weak in some sense, a stabilizing speculator would want to go short on the lira. He would then have to decide what to go long in. Now if he were in the period of the pound sterling prior to 1914, he would just go long in pounds; he wouldn't think about it. If he were in the period of the stable dollar as a riskless asset from 1945 to 1965, he would simply go long in dollars. But under the present system of floating, where we have no single national money which people view as a riskless asset,

we can't have decentralized speculation. In order for a speculator to take a position, whether long or short, in any one currency, he really has to be an expert in all currencies. I would
submit that this is an important reason for the instability in the
foreign-exchange markets that we are currently observing. If
it were possible for one currency, such as the dollar, to be stable, and if people had confidence that it was stable even though
all other currencies were inflating at different rates, people
would form anticipations of those rates of inflation, and the
hour-to-hour movements in the exchange markets would be
greatly mitigated simply because people could confidently take
positions in dollars.

Well, the upshot of all this is that what we need is not so
much an SDR or a particular money issued by an international
agency but, rather, a single stable money, whether it is national
or international.

TRIFFIN: Let me make a very brief and rather technical
comment. As I said to Marcus Fleming at lunch, the SDR "basket" cannot be used as a contractual unit for long-term contracts,
nor can it be used as a means of intervention in the exchange
market. It would be feasible, however, to use the SDR basket
as the bench mark with respect to which one can determine
which currencies remain the stablest. From this information,
one could devise a stable contractual unit and means of intervention in the market.

Chairman THORP: Let me ask a question here. You said
that the SDR basket cannot be used in long-term contracts. I
could use it for indexation, couldn't I?

TRIFFIN: You could, but you would have some problems.
One is that, whenever any single currency moves up or down in
the exchange market, the value of the whole basket is affected.
I have been proposing in Europe an arrangement along the lines
I mentioned a moment ago; it is being examined now by the
European Community and, I think, will probably be the best
hope of getting something which is stable for the largest pos-
sible number of countries.

Chairman THORP: You've stimulated a lot of interest.
Mr. Salant:

SALANT: I don't understand what Robert means when he
says that any basket can fluctuate. In relation to what?

TRIFFIN: In relation to any component currency.

FLEMING: I would like to make an observation about what
John Parke Young was saying. Some of us in the Fund have

been thinking from time to time about this question of trying
to make the SDR available for use by private individuals. One
problem which comes to mind is whether one really wants to
reproduce in a new form the problems raised by the hoarding
of gold. In other words, if private individuals can hold an asset
that is a reserve medium for central banks, there is the possibility that variations of private confidence in this asset will lead
to increases and decreases in central bank reserves. This may
not be a decisive objection, but it is one objection.

Another consideration is that, for a long time, one would
expect the private market for SDRs to be pretty thin. After
all, the SDR is not a national currency, and its use would presumably be confined to transactions by transnational firms—a
sort of replacement for the Eurocurrencies. One wonders
whether, in competition with a national currency which can be
used much more easily for transfers all over the world, the
SDR would take hold. And if it didn't take hold, if the market
didn't become sufficiently broad, could one really try to peg
national currencies to the SDR? Because, in addition to the
obligation to receive SDRs, countries would have an obligation
to make their own currencies convertible into SDRs.

TAMAGNA: I would like to ask a question of Professor
Triffin. In what way would his proposal differ from the multiple-
currency obligations which have been very common in the Eurodollar market—where you have a choice between, say, the mark,
the guilder, and the franc?

TRIFFIN: Well, there are three units which have been used
very widely in borrowing. One is the European currency unit,
which is simply an exchange option. The creditor can ask for
any currency he wants.

TAMAGNA: In some cases, three currencies have been
stipulated specifically.

TRIFFIN: Yes, but that is a very heavy gamble for the borrower. The two units which have received the most accepta-
bility are the European currency unit and the SDR unit of account.
We should not forget that such unit-of-account obligations now
total over $1 billion. But there are problems. Initially, the
SDR unit of account was defined in gold, then gold disappeared.
Then it was defined in terms of IMF parities and, later, in
terms of central rates. I would suggest defining the unit of
account as equivalent to whichever member currency remains
stablest in terms of the weighted basket of member currencies.
I have made a number of quite extensive calculations of the

nine currencies of the European Community. Since 1969, the stablest one has been the Danish krone, which has depreciated least in the whole basket. Commencing with other dates, the Belgian franc or the guilder would have been the stablest. These are actual currencies dealt with in the market and, in answer to Marcus Fleming, I think that a unit based on which- ever currency remains stablest in terms of the weighted basket would be far more attractive today than Eurodollars if one takes into account the fact that one must find not only lenders but bor- rowers. Of course, the best unit for the lender may be the D-mark.

Chairman THORP: We can hand this whole problem to the econometricians, who will doubtless come up with lots of in- teresting sheets of paper. Of course, the new unit which Bob proposes might itself affect its components! John Young, the floor is yours.

YOUNG: Bob, you said that we couldn't use the SDR for long-term contracts because, as I understood it, the basket of currencies is too unstable. But isn't it true that if we take into account the possibility of large-scale capital flows, any national currency is likely to be more unstable in the future than a basket of currencies?

TRIFFIN: I agree that the SDR is better than any national currency in terms of stability, but the unit which I propose is better than the SDR, because it would not change simply because the lira or the pound happens to change, whereas the value of the SDR basket would change whenever any single currency in the basket changes.

YOUNG: Of course, the dollar is the main currency in the basket, with a weight of one-third. A less important currency wouldn't have much effect.

TRIFFIN: That's right, but remember that a 15 percent depreciation of the dollar in terms of the D-mark, for example, would mean only a 5 percent depreciation of the SDR in terms of the D-mark.

TAMAGNA: But wouldn't your unit be unattractive to the borrower?

TRIFFIN: No, my unit offers the best protection for both creditors and debtors; it avoids both windfall profits and wind- fall losses.

WILLETT: Let me add a short remark. I commend to members an article Fritz Machlup wrote about a year ago, in which he concluded that we may move toward private usage

of the SDR without any official action. The market can roll its
own, so to speak, whether it's the European currency unit, the
SDR basket, Bob Triffin's proposal, or some other scheme.
And we've already been moving in that direction. We may get
to John Young's proposal even if we don't have any official action
along that line.

ALIBER: My comment follows from those of John Parke
Young and Tom Willett. One thing we've learned from the Euro-
banking system is that we can separate the unit-of-account function from the other traditional functions of money, and so we
must ask ourselves this question: since the Bank of America,
Security Pacific, and other participants in the Eurodollar market are free to denominate their liabilities and claims in SDRs,
why haven't they done so? In a period of great uncertainty about
future exchange rates and future interest rates, it should have
been a natural.

Chairman THORP: This I regard as a rhetorical question
and, as such, not requiring an answer. In reviewing our discussion of today, I note that there have been very few references to
the subject of gold. Now the last thing I want to do at this hour
is to open up a long discussion on that topic. Our first conference was entirely devoted to gold, which remains as controver-
sial a subject as it was in 1967. But I do think our record should
show that we are aware of recent developments in this connection, and I have asked Bob Solomon to make a brief statement
about current official thinking on the matter.

SOLOMON: Thank you, Willard, for this unhappy assign-
ment. Gold is one of the many topics on the official reform
agenda and, as we have already noted, international monetary
reform has been put on a back burner, now being regarded as
an evolutionary process —which, incidentally, doesn't necessarily imply survival of the fittest. In the discussions of the
Committee of Twenty, there was no consensus about gold except
on the general proposition that the role of both gold and the reserve currencies should decline and that the SDR should become
the central reserve asset. On that there was general agreement.
Whether you want to call it lip service or honest agreement is
up to you, but no one dissented from that proposition.

Since the Committee of Twenty was dissolved, there has
been discussion among the members of the Common Market,
some of which are anxious that transactions in gold at market-
related prices should be authorized among central banks. Under
the present Articles of Agreement of the International Monetary

Fund, no monetary authority may buy gold at a price above the
official price, plus some small margin, or may sell it below
the official price, minus some small margin. And there is still
an official price—namely, the U. S. dollar price of gold, which
is now $42.22 an ounce, whereas the market price is presently
around $175. Central banks may sell gold on the market; this
is perfectly consistent with the Fund Articles. They may also
lend gold to each other, and value the collateral at any price
they wish. We've had one such transaction between Italy and
Germany in which gold was valued at $120 an ounce.

The proposals that are circulating among Common Market
countries would provide that central banks could buy gold from,
or sell gold to, each other at any price—presumably close to
the free-market price. Central banks could, of course, sell in
the market as they do now if they wish to. After a given period,
during which there would be some restrictions on purchases, central banks would also be free to buy in the market. From the
little bit I've heard, there is less agreement among European
authorities on this particular provision than on the others. During a transitional period, which is stated to be two years, there
would be limits on purchases. I have heard this provision stated
in more ways than one. Under one version, the rule would be to
permit no net inflow of gold into the monetary system. Under a
more stringent version, no single central bank would be permitted to make a net addition to its gold through market purchases.
In any event, the limitations on purchases from the market would
have a time dimension, after which central banks presumably
could buy freely in the market.

This is a position held by a number of Europeans; I don't know
how solidly or with how much passion it is held. As for the rest
of the world, the Japanese are opposed to the whole business;
from what I know, they do not want gold to be bought or sold by
central monetary authorities at a market-related price. Most
developing countries are also opposed to the proposal and, to be
perfectly frank, the U. S. government is not agreed within itself
on the matter.

That's as objective a statement as I can make, Willard, without injecting my own strong biases on the subject.

Chairman THORP: May I suggest that, instead of continuing
this discussion here, all members who wish to pursue the subject further should sit together tomorrow at a table at lunch.

SALANT: Could I ask Bob to add a word about implications,
because he hasn't indicated any reason for interest in these

matters.

Chairman THORP: All right; the Chairman is overruled by Walter Salant.

SOLOMON: Those who are worried about the European proposals I've just described feel that once one starts down the road of authorizing central bank transactions at a much higher gold price — a market-related price —no central bank will be willing to buy at the new higher price, whatever that may be, unless it has some assurance that the market price will not fall below the price at which it buys. So the next step is likely to be some kind of formal or informal agreement among central banks to provide a new floor under the market price. This is tantamount to establishing a new official price of gold. It is because people see that as the next step that they oppose the first step. I hope this satisfies Walter.

FRANK: Isn't an additional consideration what all this means in terms of the distribution of international liquidity? Bob mentioned that Japan and the developing countries are opposed to any trend back toward gold; I take it that the reason they are opposed is that they don't have the gold. It is the countries which do have the gold—the United States and some of the continental countries —which could accommodate very nicely to the proposals Bob outlined.

TRIFFIN: This way of increasing the value of international monetary reserves would weaken the argument for issuing SDRs.

FRANK: Exactly.

Chairman THORP: In closing this session, may I suggest, first, that we have had an excellent discussion and, second, that we've produced enough chaos to provide considerable material for Lord Robbins' summary Sunday morning.

V. DEALING WITH THE DILEMMA OF STAGFLATION

Arthur B. Laffer and
Conference Members

Chairman THORP: Our topic this morning is the problem
which arises from the coincidence of inflation and depression.
As Gottfried Haberler pointed out yesterday, this problem poses
a perplexing dilemma, since measures to deal with inflation may
increase depression and unemployment, whereas measures to
reduce depression may increase inflation. I am asking Art Laffer to start the discussion by examining the extent to which inflation and recession are the result of monetary factors.

ARTHUR B. LAFFER: There are two prongs to the inflation
question: the one is the money side and the other, of course, is
the goods side. As we all know, inflation is basically a matter
of too much money chasing too few goods. And if we are talking
about world inflation, it seems quite appropriate to examine what
has happened to the world money supply.
There are several factors influencing world monetary growth.
In the first place, of course, there is the growth in domestic
money supplies—in M-1, M-2, M-3, or however we want to
define money. In the second place, exchange-rate changes can
lead to changes in the world money supply as measured in any
single currency. If, for example, the dollar depreciates by
5 percent, the dollar value of other currencies will increase
by about 5 percent, and the global money supply, as measured
in dollars, will increase by a somewhat lower percentage. Other
cases may be more complicated, but the value of the world money supply, as measured in any given currency, is in general

affected by changes in exchange rates. Of course, if we use the mark as the unit of account, the mark value of the world money supply could be declining at a time when the dollar value is increasing. There is a third important source of growth in the world money supply—namely, deposits denominated in nonlocal currencies. I am referring mainly to Eurodollar deposits, but in the last few years there has been a very rapid growth in other Eurocurrency deposits.

These three factors account for the rapid growth in the world money supply. To control global inflation, we need to fight on all three fronts; we need to restrain the growth of domestic money supplies, we need to stabilize exchange rates, and we need to control the expansion of Eurocurrencies, or "stateless money," to use Fritz Machlup's apt term.

Now for a few remarks on the other side of the equation—the goods side. If inflation is too much money chasing too few goods, we can reduce inflation either by reducing monetary expansion or by increasing output. Much has been said here about the conflict between measures to deal with recession and measures to deal with inflation; it has been said that if we cure recession, we will increase inflation, and that if we cure inflation, we will aggravate recession. This seems to me very misleading. In itself an increase in output and employment does not increase inflationary pressure; it reduces it. What we need to do in order to reduce world inflation is to increase as much as we can world production of goods and services.

But there is a big obstacle. In the last five or ten years, a great separation has occurred between reward and effort. In the United States, for example, we have had a very rapid growth of transfer payments; we've driven a big wedge between wages paid and wages received. This wedge has tended to reduce output and employment both on the demand side and on the supply side. Firms hire labor on the basis of total wages paid; the more they have to pay, the less labor they hire. Workers are induced to work on the basis of the net wages they actually receive; the less they get, the less they will work. Thus this growing wedge between wages paid and wages received has tended to reduce world output and employment while at the same time increasing world inflation. The wedge has increased very rapidly, not only in the United States, but also in other countries, such as Great Britain.

The moral, of course, is to reduce the wedge. We need to decrease transfer payments and to decrease taxes in order to get the stimulative fiscal effects necessary to increase output. At the same time, of course, we should do whatever is neces- sary to gain control over the world money supply and, in par- ticular, to reduce its rate of growth.

HENRY C. WALLICH: I would like to ask Art a question. Does he take it for granted that an increase in taxes reduces the supply of labor? Doesn't that depend on the interaction be- tween the average tax and the marginal tax? The average tax increases the labor supply; the marginal tax reduces it. As a result, if, as in the United States, we finance social security with a low marginal tax which is equal, in effect, to the average tax, I wonder whether the effect on the supply of labor isn't at least neutral—or even positive.

LAFFER: Well, of course, what we should be looking at are the marginal tax rates overall, which in the United States and Britain are very high relative to average tax rates. For the social-security tax alone, the wedge is about 12 percent.

Chairman THORP: Percent of what, Art?

LAFFER: Of payrolls. And the average rate is almost equal to the marginal rate in the case of social security. If you look at the net benefits received in relation to taxes paid, you find that the marginal tax rate increases quite substantially. In other words, once you become a member of the system, your social-security benefits do not increase in proportion to your social-security payments.

WALLICH: That isn't quite right either, Art, because peo- ple expect social security to be greatly upgraded during their lifetime. That is to say, under present rules they indeed get less than they pay in, knowing that by the time they retire they will get much more than they put in. Everybody knows that by the time they retire—unless they are about to retire—they will get much more than what the law now says.

LAFFER: If everybody knows that, I think they're in for a big shock.

DE CECCO: Art Laffer's theory is similar to what in OECD circles is sometimes called the "Nordic" theory—the Swedish or Norwegian theory—of inflation. As he put it today, the prob- lem looks very simple; we reduce transfer payments, and then firms find it profitable to hire more people. But there are some firms for which the transfer payments are an important source of demand. In such cases, a reduction in transfer pay- ments may reduce employment. So we have a problem of aggre- gation; we have to see what the net result is. The matter is not as simple as Art implies: he has to prove his case.

McKINNON: My comment is inspired by the remarks of Art Laffer and Henry Wallich. In discussing the effect of transfer payments on the supply of labor, we are not really dealing with pure transfer payments in the sense that recipients of the payments can then go ahead and decide whether or not to participate in the labor force; a large number of these transfer payments actually pay people to stay out of the labor force. I am referring not only to retired people who can no longer enter the labor force without losing their social-security benefits but also to people covered by welfare programs of one sort or another. The point I am making is that we are not looking at some kind of neutral transfer payment from one group to another and then worrying about their propensity to participate in the labor force as determined by their level of income; we are actually paying people to stay out of the labor market in a wide variety of circumstances. In effect, unemployment insurance fits into this category if it is indefinitely extended.

Chairman THORP: Art, there are several members who want to get into this discussion; instead of dealing with each individually, I suggest that you reply to them all at a later point. The first is Bob Aliber.

ALIBER: Let me ask Art whether inflations always result from this wedge between wages paid and wages received, and whether, in this respect, there is something really unique in the last several years. Is this feature of world inflation actually independent of what is happening to the money supply?

SOHMEN: On the same point, it seems to me that, in the abstract, one can make a case that increased social-security payments may reduce the willingness to work and reduce the productivity of the economy, but I am not sure that the empirical evidence supports such a conclusion. Most of Western Europe has a vastly more extensive social-security system than the United States. This is true of Germany, for example, and you would not claim that Germans show any signs of not working hard enough. Or would you?

FLEMING: Art Laffer's line of thought is not very familiar to me; I'm still steeped in Keynesianism. I would like to ask whether his theory of labor supply is based on the assumption of collective bargaining or of the individual supply of labor. If it is based on the individual's willingness or desire to work, then let us not forget about the backward-sloping supply curve which is often found in this area. If Art assumes collective bargaining, then I don't think he can derive simple theorems from the individual sphere; he has to look at what is actually happening—at the kind of factors that influence the outcome of collective bargaining. This, I suspect, is a much more complicated question than Art has allowed for.

HABERLER: At our opening session yesterday, I said that the coexistence of recession and inflation poses a nasty dilemma; if we fight inflation by tightening money, we intensify recession, and if we fight recession by easier money, we intensify inflation. Now Art Laffer says the opposite is true: if we fight recession, we also fight inflation. What he has in mind is that we can increase output by some gimmick—the one he mentioned or some other one. I fully agree that if we can get people to work harder and produce more without an increase in the money supply and without an expansionary fiscal policy, we are much better off so far as inflation is concerned. I have a certain sympathy for the theory of the wedge, but I don't think the wedge is something that we can reduce very fast. Reducing the wedge would take years, and may not be politically or socially possible. The recession and the inflation are realities right now, and therefore I think it is still true that we have our dilemma: the ordinary fiscal and monetary policies against recession intensify inflation, and vice versa.

I do not say that the dilemma cannot be resolved. In the end, it has to be resolved—and here I agree with Marina Whitman—by microeconomic policies. Just reflect that if we had a really free competitive economy, including a competitive labor market, stagflation would be impossible. Thus the ultimate resolution of the dilemma must come through microeconomic policies.

One word about the world money supply. I think one can speak of a world money supply under fixed exchange rates, but under flexible exchange rates the concept breaks down. For example, as Art Laffer admitted, if the dollar is depreciating, the world money supply in terms of dollars goes up, but the world money supply in terms of marks at the same time may be going down. So I don't think that the world money supply is a useful concept in a situation of general floating.

SCHMIDT: My point relates to the observations of Art Laffer and Ronald McKinnon. As a result of the work of Martin Feldstein in the last three or four years, I was stimulated to do a study on unemployment compensation for the Commonwealth of Virginia. The important thing to remember is that unemployment benefits are tax-free, whereas the income that a man receives from working is subject to federal, state, and sometimes local taxes, as well as social-security payments. What I discovered from the actual 1973 data for Virginia was that if a man was unemployed for three months, his income, after all taxes were deducted, fell by only 10 percent when he went on the unemployment rolls. There are anecdotes of workers with high seniority who preferred to be laid off first rather than last, simply because this was a way of financing a vacation. Thus there is considerable empirical evidence, at least in Virginia, for the kind of thing that Ronald McKinnon was talking about.

Let me add another word on world money supply. As I understand it, the U.S. money supply cannot be affected by international transactions under a regime of completely floating exchange rates. Barring official intervention in the exchange market and barring certain shifts in funds between commercial banks and the Fed, international transactions do not affect the U.S. monetary base or the U.S. money supply. Thus I don't see how money supplies in other countries are relevant to U.S. inflation.

TRIFFIN: My remark is on the point just made by Wilson Schmidt. He may be right with respect to the United States in the sense that there has been relatively little official intervention in the exchange market, although there is some now. But for other countries, intervention has been a major element. Moreover, the depreciation of the dollar has increased the dollar value of world monetary reserves by about 22 percent. Even when expressed in SDRs—that is, abstracting from dollar depreciation—world reserves have increased by 130 percent; they have more than doubled. Then, of course, we also have to keep in mind the tremendous growth of Eurocurrency deposits. All of these factors affect high-powered reserve money, which in terms of total money supply is multiplied again by a factor ranging from 2.5 to 3. Even under floating, there has been an increase in the last year of 20 percent in high-powered money resulting from the flooding of the system by reserve currencies.

Chairman THORP: Let me interrupt a moment. You mentioned three things which increase the world supply of money; you did not include SDRs. I take it that you don't regard the SDR as money—just as a reserve.

LAFFER: The SDR does, of course, affect the money supply by increasing the monetary base.

TRIFFIN: I would agree that the creation of SDRs has been a source of world inflation. But I would like to remind people of the order of magnitude: a $9 billion increase in SDRs; a $100 billion increase in reserve currencies. It is really ridiculous to imply that these two sources are of comparable importance.

SOLOMON: Let me go back to Art Laffer's remarks on world money supply. He apparently wants to add Eurocurrency deposits to the world total of M-1. But many Eurocurrency deposits are interest-bearing; they are not M-1 as we define the term in the United States. Why doesn't Art include savings-and-loan association deposits, building-society deposits, and all sorts of other interest-bearing liquid assets? Why is he so selective in his choice of monetary variables? His definition of world money seems a little inconsistent, I must say.

McCLELLAN: My remarks are related to those of Ronald McKinnon and Wilson Schmidt on the impact of welfare costs on inflation. In the United States, as elsewhere, our public welfare programs tend to outrun our resources. Powerful groups put political pressure behind many different programs. We wind up with a wide variety of costly social services which are self-perpetuating and under which truly needy citizens often receive little or no help, while large groups with political clout draw extravagant benefits. One of the main difficulties is that, historically, the United States Congress has never considered as two parts of one problem both budget expenditures and the taxes required to pay for them. As a result, federal expenditures have increased much more rapidly than federal receipts, and the deficit has been largely financed by excessive creation of money. This, to my mind, has been a major cause of inflation both here and throughout the world.

SCITOVSKY: My brief comment is inspired by Art Laffer's wedge theory. Consider, for example, the rise in the price of oil. This reduces real income, prompting labor to press for higher wages. To the extent that we then have a reduction in employment, the unemployed labor is able to go on welfare and to continue to draw income in the form of transfer payments. The decline in output makes the inflation worse, and the process is self-perpetuating.

SILK: It seems to me that any government which finances its activities by taxes creates wedges all over the place. I frequently get letters from people who say that the way to deal with inflation is to reduce taxes on business; all we have to do

is to reduce the wedge between income earned and income received and, lo, our problem is solved—for example, via an
increase in capital formation. But I submit that this is too
simple a way of looking at things. What one has to do is to
look at the ultimate flows into and out of government and the
particular programs that are involved. This is not to say that
all government expenditures are justified, but it seems to me
that we cannot talk about these matters in such a narrow context as a wedge—that's what a tax is; it's a wedge.

Lord ROBBINS: May I toss just this one observation into
the arena. I speak of conditions in my own country, where
there are wedges all over the place. But I humbly submit that
the growth in output which could result from a reduction—a conceivable reduction—of these wedges would be negligible compared to the growth in output which could result from a reduction
of restrictive practices.

JAMISON: My point overlaps the point made by Mr. McClellan, but I would like to make it anyway. Mention has been made
here from time to time of the weakness of the dollar. A major
reason for that weakness must be the general awareness of the
huge deficits, present and prospective, in our federal budget.
For 1975-76, the deficit could well be $75-100 billion; you pick
your own figure. Most of this deficit will be monetized, providing inflationary fuel when the economic recovery is under
way. Thus inflation, which is currently showing an encouraging subsidence in the United States, may well show a major
resurgence later. I don't wish to imply that a deficit is inappropriate at this time, but it appears to me that the panic in
Washington over recession is causing fiscal excesses which
may later lead to a high price in inflation.

WHITMAN: One quick comment on this question of the relationship between the size of the U.S. budget deficit and the
weakness or strength of the dollar. Presumably, that deficit
will be distributed in some way among an increase in output,
an increase in interest rates, and an increase in the rate of
inflation. Only one of these three effects, I would say, would
contribute to the weakness of the dollar—that is, an increase
in the rate of U.S. inflation relative to the rate of inflation
abroad. To the extent that the deficit raises interest rates, it
would tend, other things being equal, to strengthen the dollar
in the exchange markets. So it is by no means obvious that the
size of the deficit will lead to a weakening of the dollar; it's a
much more ambivalent question.

WILLETT: Let me add a word to what Marina Whitman has said. It would seem to me that, in the very short term, if a budget deficit had any effect on the exchange market, it would be in the direction of appreciation of the country's currency because of the effects that Marina mentioned. The increase in interest rates resulting from the budget deficit would probably come first, and initially that would likely dominate longer-run effects that might operate in the other direction.

TRIFFIN: This is another brief remark on Marina's statement. If I remember correctly, the 1971 calendar U.S. budget deficit was about $25 billion. We all learned from our textbooks that if a deficit is financed by borrowing from the public, that is all right; if it is financed by the commercial banks, it begins to smell; and if it is financed by the Federal Reserve, it is much worse. Well, we escaped all that because we borrowed $30 billion from foreign central banks and commercial banks. We all know what impact this had on inflation in the United States, on inflation abroad, and on the dollar.

WALLICH: I would like to ask Robert a couple of questions. In his observations about world monetary reserves, shouldn't he point out that the reserves accumulated by OPEC countries are not really in the same category as reserves of other countries but are the precursor to longer-term investment? And how should one look at gold? The reserve role of gold could be viewed by countries as ranging all the way from zero to its full value at the market price. Because of the ambiguous gold situation, one really doesn't know whether countries think they are rich or poor in reserves.

Chairman THORP: Perhaps you should answer Henry now, Bob, as the points he raises are very important.

TRIFFIN: I quite agree. As for the treatment of the reserves of the OPEC countries, of course much more needs to be said. For the moment, I would simply say that we cannot just exclude OPEC reserves from the total or consider that they have no weight in the whole business. With respect to gold, I am quite sure that no central bank really considers its gold holdings on the basis of the official valuation at $42 an ounce. But what figure to use instead of that is another question; one has to look at the situation from day to day, perhaps valuing the gold at some arbitrary minimum figure based on the market price.

FLEMING: My comment is related to Robert's proposition that the enormous expansion of reserves is creating base money, enabling a big superstructure of monetary expansion to take place. Now it seems to me, unless I'm greatly mistaken, that nothing like a proportionate expansion of money has occurred following the big expansion of reserves from 1970 onward. In various ways, central banks have prevented a proportionate expansion of money. Similarly, the big current expansion of reserves in the oil countries has not resulted in a proportionate expansion of domestic money supplies, or anything like it.

SOLOMON: Well, as long as we're attacking Robert Triffin as well as Art Laffer, may I make a comment?

Chairman THORP: Yes; Art Laffer is getting a little rest at the moment.

SOLOMON: Robert has referred several times to the big increase in reserve currencies in the last four years. His facts are correct, of course, but I think one needs to look at the background. I'm wondering if he would accept the following propositions.

First, a good part of the creation of reserve currencies in the last four years was the result of the breakdown of the system—a breakdown which Robert himself predicted back in the late 1950s. The predicted event finally happened, beginning in 1970-71, and there was an enormous outpouring of speculative funds from the United States. This flow was not a part of the normal working of the system; it was a result of the breakdown of the system.

Second, a significant part of the growth of dollar reserves arises from the fact that some central banks, particularly in the developing countries (including the OPEC countries) have placed their reserves in the Euromarket. This has led to a multiplication of reserves which is a reflection neither of the sins of the United States nor of the breakdown of the system but of certain practices in reserve holdings which automatically increase reserves. I suspect that Henry Wallich's comment is consistent with what I am about to say, though I don't always feel forced to agree with my colleague.

Chairman THORP: But it's a good idea!

SOLOMON: Quite so. In any case, I suspect that if, as Henry suggests, we regard OPEC dollar holdings as foreign investments rather than as reserves, there probably has been very little reserve creation in the past year.

SALANT: My comment is concerned with Triffin's argument that the increase in reserves has been a cause of the increase in money supplies and therefore of world inflation.

If we look at the situation country by country, we find that the countries with the biggest reserve increases didn't have the biggest increases in their money supplies. Moreover, some of the countries with big increases in money supplies didn't have big reserve increases. This suggests that there is a good deal more to be explained than can be derived from Robert's simple theory. It would appear that the countries with big increases in money supply had them because of their domestic policies, whereas the countries that had received the big reserve increases took steps to offset them.

Chairman THORP: If there are no further shots at Robert, he can reply to his critics now, after which we can turn back to our other target, Art Laffer.

TRIFFIN: Marcus Fleming has pointed out that a number of countries have tried to offset the inflow of monetary reserves and that, as a result, the expansion of national money supplies has been at a much lower rate than the expansion of reserves. This is perfectly true. If we look at Germany, for instance, the increase in money supply during the period 1970-73 was only about $10 billion, whereas the inflow of reserves was $26 billion; thus there was a considerable degree of sterilization on the part of Germany. On the other hand, as Walter Salant pointed out, the opposite has been true in certain countries. During the same period, the French money supply increased by $24 billion, of which only $5 billion was from the inflow of reserves. In the Italian case, a $47 billion increase in the money supply was accompanied by only a $1 billion increase in reserves. And in the United Kingdom—in an intermediate position—an $11 billion increase in the money supply was $7 billion greater than the increase in reserves.

There is no doubt that all this needs to be looked at much more carefully. The aggregates, I think, are still significant even when we take into account the matter of petrodollars. It is true that we can regard these dollars as Arab investments, but the fact is that the dollars held by the Arabs may later be spent, thus increasing the reserves of the rest of the world. For the time being, one can think of petrodollars as an investment, but it is an investment which remains liquid and can be used to cover a balance-of-payments deficit.

I'm not trying to assign blame in this whole business. If I were to do so, I would have to assign part of it to the countries which have accepted dollars in order to avoid appreciation of their currencies. But the United States would not have had such enormous payments deficits if it had not been for the Vietmanese war.

Chairman THORP: I think we should now return to the issues raised by Art Laffer.

ARNDT: I have a short question for Art. Governments impose wedges to further various aims. Art wishes to remove these wedges because he wants to achieve certain ends regarding inflation and unemployment. If removing or reducing the wedges makes it more difficult to further other ends, what then will happen to those ends? How would Art make decisions as to what shall be given up and what shall be retained?

KOHLHAGEN: Just one quick empirical question. I would like to ask Art if his theory implies that the larger the wedge, the greater the upward pressure on prices as a long-run effect. Has he observed this empirically?

HINSHAW: I have a rather big question for Art Laffer, whose name is often linked with that of Robert Mundell, who couldn't be with us. I should point out that, an hour before our reception on Thursday, I received a telegram from Bob in which he said that urgent business prevented him from being here. He coupled this information with a request that I please emphasize to all of you the need for a $60 billion tax cut combined with tight money! Without implying any position on this clearly heroic approach to the problem of stagflation, it seems to me that if a large budget deficit is to occur in a setting of tight money, this means that the resulting debt must not be monetized; in other words, the government must borrow from the private sector—surely at quite high interest rates. Under such conditions, I wonder whether there would be much stimulation of output and employment or, at any rate, much stimulation via an increase in private investment. I've asked Bob about this before, but have never received a very clear answer. If Art could help us out, it would be most useful.

Chairman THORP: There are two kinds of paintings that everyone has noticed in wandering through art galleries. There are the heroes who, with their shields, manage to avert all arrows that come in their direction, and there are the martyrs who accumulate arrows. We shall now find out where to classify Art Laffer.

LAFFER: Whether I'm a hero or a martyr, you will have to judge. I'm trying to remember all the arrows that have been directed at me, though I shall probably forget the questions I can't answer.

First, let me say that although social security accounts for a large fraction of transfer payments in the United States, there are many other forms — agricultural subsidies not to produce, Medicare, Medicaid, and food stamps, to name a few. A recent example of a large transfer payment was the rebate on last year's income taxes. A tax rebate is a transfer payment based on last year's income, and has nothing to do with labor services currently performed.

In discussing transfer payments, let me emphasize that the economic effects are sharply different from the effects of government purchases of goods and services to meet public needs. Unlike transfer payments, government purchases do not involve a separation of work from income.

In response to Bob Aliber's skeptical observation about the uniqueness of the present situation, I would simply say that we do find ourselves in a radically altered setting as compared with a few years back. The increase in transfer payments in the United States over the last ten years has been really astounding. Social-security benefits, for example, have been growing at a rate of about $10 billion a year, and are now around $70 billion annually. Even as late as 1969, the social-security program was small compared to what it is now. Most of the other programs —food stamps, Medicare, Medicaid, and so on— are very recent.

On another matter, Bob Solomon criticized me for including Eurodeposits in the world money supply, because they earn interest whereas M-1 does not. This does not seem to me a very important question. In the studies we have done at the University of Chicago, we used M-1 for national money supplies because it's the easiest figure to obtain, but I would have no objection to using M-2 or some broader measure.

Now for a word on Bob Mundell's dramatic telegram. Bob's position now, as I understand it, is that many tax rates are currently prohibitive and that if we reduce these tax rates we will increase total revenue instead of reducing it. At the same time, by encouraging investment, we can also increase output and employment—the increase in output tending to restrain inflation. Personally, I don't know whether Bob is right or not, but I find him difficult to refute.

Chairman THORP: Leonard Silk has asked for the floor; I hope that he's not resuming the debate with Art Laffer.

SILK: I'm not debating; I'm just making a plea for technical improvement in language. We should distinguish sharply between a reduction in tax rates and a reduction in tax revenue. Under some conditions, a cut in tax rates could lead to an increase in tax revenue. The point is that we need to be careful about how we define a tax cut.

SOLOMON: I would like to get back to the inflation-recession question. The first point I would stress is that we are not now in a situation of excess demand for major products anywhere in the industrialized world. Frank Tamagna reminded me yesterday that in some rural areas there may be excess demand; he's having difficulty getting people to build a house for him in rural Italy, and he has my sympathy, but I don't think we should generalize too much from that particular case.

TAMAGNA: Unemployment varies greatly here in the United States. Texas has 3.5 percent unemployment; in Detroit, the figure is several times as high. In every country, there is some situation like that.

SOLOMON: I was trying to bow to your point before you interrupted. My main point is that we are in a world situation of inadequate demand, yet prices are continuing to rise at a disturbing rate. The price advances clearly are not a result of excess demand but of something else—namely, rising costs mainly in the form of wage costs. The big question is whether attempts to reduce unemployment by stimulating demand will aggravate these cost-push forces that exist in varying degrees of intensity in the industrialized countries. If the answer is yes, there is a strong case, as Lord Robbins indicated in his opening address, for the temporary use of incomes policies. There isn't much doubt that the world situation is serious enough to call for stimulative policies on the fiscal and monetary side. The problem is to stimulate demand at a rate which is sustainable and which doesn't push us through the ceiling again two or three years from now.

SCITOVSKY: Just one single comment—a correction of Bob Solomon's language. He said that the present inflation is not a case of excess demand. I think that we ought to distinguish between excess demand in the sense of demand exceeding capacity and excess demand in the sense of demand exceeding supply. I would agree with Bob that the present inflation is not of the type where demand exceeds capacity. But I'm much less certain that the present inflation is not of the kind which is due to demand exceeding the available supply as produced by an underemployed labor force and underutilized industrial equipment. This distinction, I think, is important.

GORDON K. DOUGLASS: Bob Solomon has suggested that most of our present inflation is caused by rising costs rather than by excess demand. I am wondering whether our policy recommendations on how to stimulate economic activity while not stimulating further inflation shouldn't be predicated on some set of assumptions about what is going to happen to commodity prices in the future. That in part is a question about petroleum prices. It seems to me that some assumption is also needed about whether non-oil producers are likely to form new OPEC-type arrangements and start playing that game. I'm not sure, Mr. Chairman, whether this is the time to talk about these matters or whether you wish to reserve them for our discussion of supply factors.

Chairman THORP: I think that the matters you raise should come up when we discuss the OPEC issue this afternoon, though one of the problems of this conference is that, like most economic matters, everything involves everything else.

The Chairman will yield himself one minute to ask a question. We have had a telegram which suggests that $60 billion is the right number to produce the economic stimulation needed in connection with the recession. Now economists have come through with all sorts of numbers, and I don't think that we should get into the numbers game, but I do think that we should consider what we should look at in order to derive sensible numbers — other than picking a number out of a hat, or averaging everybody's numbers, or taking a bigger or smaller number than anybody else. There must be a way of looking at the problem that justifies a particular number. I would be very interested if Bob Solomon would make an effort to answer the question and then let the rest of us join in if we have anything to add.

SOLOMON: I have a very short reply to that. I don't plan to provide you with a number, but in answering what one should look at, I should point out that I am an old Keynesian. We have known for years the fact that the budget responds to the economy as well as the fact that the economy responds to the budget. That bit of understanding is embodied in a concept known as the full-employment (or high-employment) budget, which, depending on conditions, can be in surplus or in deficit. As an analytical device, the concept is useful because it helps us to estimate the proper magnitude of the budget deficit that some people worry about and other people think is too small. The only answer I would give to your question, Mr. Chairman, is to concentrate

on some form of high-employment budget position in order to
evaluate the stimulus that is contained in various fiscal proposals.

Lord ROBBINS: Might I ask a question which arises from
my ignorance of the quantitative magnitudes commonly enter-
tained in discussions in this country: what percentage of unemployment is a high-employment situation?

SOLOMON: Well, there have been arguments about this, sir;
you can pick your own level and make your own calculations. If
you prefer 4 percent, then you can calculate it at 4 percent; if
you prefer 5 percent, you can calculate it at 5 percent. But the
important variable is the change over time in this high-employment budget position.

SALANT: Bob Solomon has pointed out one of the things we
need to know in trying to decide how much expansion we should
have. But he hasn't really dealt with the dilemma which he himself posed— namely, how much is too much in the sense that it
conflicts with the purpose of reducing the degree of price rise.
We simply don't know how much expansion we could have with a
given degree of price rise until we know how much of the price
rise is attributable to lags from past increases in the prices of
inputs. When Lord Robbins opened the conference, he referred
to the possibility, when talking about inflation, that much of the
price rise that goes on at any given moment is due to lags.
Well, I would like to suggest that much of the price rise we've
had in the past few months —perhaps all of it—has been due to
such lags. Here, of course, we must distinguish between the
consumer-price index, which continues to rise, and the whole-
sale-price index, which recently has actually been declining.

The point of all this is that we can't begin to know how much
a given expansion will affect prices until we know how much of
the current price rise is due to things that are just registering
now but are responses to things that happened in the past. If
the estimates are right, it would take about three years, even
with a 7 percent rate of growth in real output, before unemployment moved down to 5 percent. If this is so, it would seem
quite possible to me that we could have a considerable degree
of expansion without much increase in the rate of price rise.
On the other hand, if the consumer-price index is only going to
get down to an annual rate of increase of 6 percent at the bottom
of the present decline, there is reason to wonder if that isn't an
awfully high rate from which to begin a new expansion.

Lord ROBBINS: It is beginning to sound as if you are arguing that the lags will work themselves out and that there will be
no further influence in an upward direction.

SALANT: I'm arguing that this is a possibility which should
be looked into. I'm not sure of it; that is why I say that a 6 percent rate of price increase is an awfully high rate from which
to start a new expansion. The first view I mentioned—the opti-
mistic view—is that there is a large volume of unutilized labor
and plant capacity; therefore don't worry: we can have an expansion going on for quite a few years. I'm not claiming to know
which of these two views is the correct one, but I am arguing
that we can't begin to know the answer until we know something
more about the lags.

Chairman THORP: In a sense, wouldn't your statement imply that what is important is to turn things in the right direction?
As I understand you, you don't think in terms of a "gap" to be
filled but of a changed set of forces.

SALANT: Well, what I'm essentially arguing is that we need
to know more about the time distribution of the lags of quite a
few things, including the rate at which the price increases of
input factors get through to the consumer-price index.

Chairman THORP: I apologize for the Chairman getting
into this. Leonard Silk:

SILK: In talking about inflation, I would like to stress the
necessity to distinguish between relative-price changes and an
overall inflationary trend. I am thinking of the quadrupling—
quintupling, actually—of oil prices and of all the international
disequilibrium which has resulted from that. For various reasons, other commodity prices have also gone up sharply, so
I'm not speaking only of oil. Now theoretically, as some economists are fond of emphasizing, these price increases do not
necessarily result in a situation that has to be resolved in an
inflationary direction. But the fact is that, thus far, the situation has been resolved in that direction, and it may have to be
in the future as well. There are downward rigidities in wages
and prices all over the place. We have had very rapid increases
in farm prices, and we are now in the process of watching
Congress go through motions to make sure that farm prices
don't come down very much. But this means that we are confronted with a relative-price adjustment which results in an
inflationary price movement. If prices are free to go up but
not to come down, no other result is possible.

JAMISON: Reference was made by Bob Solomon to the concept of a full-employment budget. Of course there are many arguments in favor of that notion which are politically popular. It should be pointed out, however, that while the concept has often been put into practice as a means of stimulating the economy, it has seldom, if ever, been applied as a means of restraint. So it is a ratchet-like policy, politically and practically; it has been followed only in one direction, never in the other.

WALLICH: I would like to comment on something that Leonard Silk seemed about to say, but then didn't say. In any case, it is a remark that is frequently made—namely, that when we face a jump in the price level because of something like the higher price of oil or the higher price of food, we should accommodate these developments by monetary policy and then go on from there. The problem with that policy, which is often recommended, is that once it is translated into higher living costs, it also gets built into wage increases; and once it's built into wage increases, it continues with a life of its own. So the argument to accommodate these one-shot commodity price increases is, I think, a dangerous one.

KOHLHAGEN: My point is on the same subject. In dealing with externally induced relative-price shocks, such as the drastic increase in the oil price, monetary authorities have shown a strong preference for permitting these shocks to be reflected in inflation rather than in declining output and employment. Now if the authorities, through monetary expansion, validate such exogenous shocks, allowing the adjustment to come mainly through a higher price level rather than through declining employment, it should not surprise us that, if they don't carry this policy far enough, we should wind up with some of the adjustment in both forms—in other words, we should wind up with stagflation.

SOHMEN: I would like to shift to a somewhat different topic, though still within the area which we are discussing. I find it rather surprising that, in a discussion of this kind, hardly anybody ever mentions the issue of antitrust policy and the possible contribution it could make to stabilization of the economy. I think the evidence that we have, not only from the United States but also from some other countries, is rather suggestive. In the recent discussion of stagflation in the United States, one could easily get the impression that this is an entirely new phenomenon, but I think most of you will remember that the United States had precisely the same trouble in the late 1950s.

As now, prices were rising at a time of deepening stagnation. The only difference I can see is that the present situation is somewhat more extreme.

In any discussion of possible action, we should differentiate between short-term and long-term objectives. As a short-run measure, I would be all in favor of more expansionary fiscal policy at the present time. But we should not lose sight of something more fundamental—namely, that we simply do not have sufficient price flexibility. There have been various suggestions on how to cope with this problem, most of which have been directed toward greater wage flexibility—or, rather, toward preventing wage increases which are considered excessive. But it seems to me that we should also devote considerably more attention to the flexibility of prices. The problem is that, for most people, antitrust policy falls into one compartment and labor-union policy falls into another. I do not see much difference between the two; in both areas, the objective should be to increase flexibility by whatever means we can find.

This issue has been clouded over by the traditional Keynesian bias that operates under the assumption of a constant price level and a constant wage level. Under this assumption, macroeconomic policies are the only means of regulating the level of employment. But if we start from a more classical model, we are confronted with the rather obvious fact that, in a world of perfect price flexibility and a high degree of competition, there would not be any involuntary unemployment in the first place.

In comparing different economies, we can learn quite a bit in this respect. A rather obvious comparison, for example, would be the performance of the British economy and that of the West German economy. One element which I think has been very important in the performance of the German economy is precisely that it is a more competitive economy than almost any other—including, I believe, the U. S. economy. I'm struck by the fact that most American economists still seem to think of Germany as a cartel paradise, which it was during the 1920s and 1930s. But the postwar situation in West Germany has been vastly different—one of the great revolutions in the history of economic policy. I think it ought to be looked at much more closely.

JOHN PARKE YOUNG: We have listened to several approaches to the problem of stagflation, and we are all agreed that our present tools for dealing with inflation and unemployment are

very slow and indirect.   In this connection, I have been working on a proposal which would influence aggregate demand by
greatly increasing the number of excise taxes.   Such taxes
would be selective—high on luxuries and graduated down to zero
on necessities.   The President would have the authority, within
agreed limits, to make across-the-board reductions or increases
in these taxes so that aggregate expenditure could be immediately
increased or reduced, as needed.   In order to make the proposal
acceptable to Congress, Congress could be authorized—say, within a period of 60 days—to veto such decreases or increases in
the excise-tax level.

This proposal would make it possible to deal promptly both
with recession and with adverse price developments.   But apart
from that, it would stand on its own feet by helping to restruc-
ture the content of our gross national product in a more rational
way.   We've produced too many of the wrong things.   My proposal would assist in improving the composition of the GNP while
at the same time giving the President the power to deal promptly
with the problems that we have been talking about.   By reducing
the excise taxes during a period of stagflation, the President
would be effectively fighting both high prices and unemployment;
he would be simultaneously lowering the cost of living and stimulating output and employment.

Chairman THORP: Our time for this session is almost over,
but before concluding our discussion of stagflation and of the
various ways of dealing with it, I think it would be useful to
spend a few more minutes on the experience of Germany, a
country which has been more successful than most in coping
with inflation and unemployment.   Egon Sohmen has already
made some remarks on this subject, and I am asking him to
speak first.

SOHMEN: All of us are aware that the West German economy
has produced large export surpluses, apparently no matter what
happens.   Whether exchange rates remain constant or whether
the mark has appreciated, Germany has for many years been
able to generate these rather remarkable export surpluses.
Some people explain this as being due to the industrial structure
of the West German economy which, simply by good fortune, has
specialized in products for which world demand has been brisk
throughout the postwar years.   Of course this can be advanced
as an explanation, but it seems to me that there is a great similarity between the German economy and the British economy,
where the story has been very different.   Thus one of the most

interesting questions in modern economic history is why these
two countries should have developed so differently, Britain having had about twice the German real income per capita in 1950
and now, twenty-five years later, Germany having twice the
British real income per capita.

Clearly, there are several reasons for the difference in the
performance of these two countries. I would certainly not neg-
lect the behavior of the British trade unions as compared with
German trade unions, though I am increasingly impressed that
the labor unions in most countries seem to mirror to a large
degree the attitudes and behavior of management in those countries. From what we know, or at least believe we know, the
British economy on the whole is still not a very competitive
economy, and this feature is reflected in trade-union behavior.
On the German side, there is a common impression that labor
unions are very weak, but I do not think this is really true.
The presently ruling Social Democratic Party, as in most other
countries, is largely identified with the labor unions, and membership levels in the unions are rather high. The biggest union,
the metal-workers union, has a membership level of about 97
percent of the working force of the industries it represents. In
other sectors, the percentage is lower, but I certainly would
not say that labor unions are a weak political or economic force
in West Germany.

But there is a striking difference in union behavior. German
labor unions seem to act in much greater awareness of the employment effects of excessive wage demands. One reason for
this, I think, is that it is very evident to them that German bus-
inesses face intense competition on the product market, so that
any attempt to raise wages too much can be done only at the risk
of unemployment.

This brings me back to the subject of industrial competition.
As I said earlier, American economists still seem to have a
picture of the West German economy as a cartel paradise, but
this situation has changed by 180 degrees since the war. Here
I would point not only to the anti-cartel legislation that was introduced after the war but also to German entry into the Common Market. I made a comparison some time ago between the
behavior of prices and rates of capacity utilization in the Com-
Market steel industry and the corresponding behavior in the
American steel industry, and obtained information from which
one could make a very convincing demonstration that competition in the steel market must be much more intense in Western

Europe than in the United States. In the United States, steel prices during the period I studied continued to go up whether demand was brisk or stagnant, whereas in the Common Market steel prices fluctuated a great deal and capacity utilization was always more or less constant at about 90 percent—which is really full-capacity utilization. In the United States, by way of contrast, there are large fluctuations, not in the price of steel, but in capacity utilization. For me this is rather convincing evidence that, at least in this one important sector, West Germany and the Common Market as a whole are more competitive than the United States.

Taking this and other evidence into account, I have come to the conclusion that the United States is no longer the country where one could say that competition is most intense as a result of forceful antitrust legislation. West Germany is now a better example of vigorous antitrust policy. I think this is the only convincing explanation for the fact that German exports did not seem to suffer much from appreciation of the mark; prices were simply adjusted sufficiently to be able to compete with the rest of the world economy.

ALIBER: Egon, I found your remarks fascinating—a wonderful commercial for Germany and for German antitrust policy. But I don't think you've explained why the mark has tended to appreciate or why the appreciation of the mark has not led to a reduction of the export surplus, as one would expect who has read your book.

SOHMEN: Well, in the first place, the effect of a change in the exchange rate can only be measured by a comparison with what would have happened if the rate had not changed. If the mark had not appreciated, the German export surpluses would doubtless have been even greater. In the second place, as I pointed out, appreciation of the mark has always gone hand in hand with a reduction in the rate of price increase in Germany. I think these events are less difficult to explain than is usually supposed.

SOLOMON: Fascinating questions have been raised by what Egon has just told us, and I would like to pursue a bit further the matter raised by Bob Aliber. Egon mentioned that, owing to the intense competition in Germany which he described so well, German companies have reduced their prices when the mark has appreciated in order to remain competitive. My first question is, what happened to profit margins of German companies in those circumstances? I would be surprised if there

were not some sort of squeeze on profits. My second question
is this: to what extent could one attribute the recent strong
trade surplus (and current-account surplus) of Germany to what
some people would call excessive contraction of domestic demand, leading German producers to look abroad for markets
because of inadequate domestic markets? I am deliberately
putting that question provocatively.

SOHMEN: On your first question, profit margins certainly
were compressed, as far as I know, each time the mark appreciated. But there had been huge profits before. The German
trade unions somehow did not fully anticipate the extent to which
inflation was being imported during the years of the adjustable
peg, and so German wages always lagged behind. So, before
each revaluation of the mark, profits were really very high, and
could stand being compressed somewhat. I should add that many
German export industries produce commodities for which demand
can't suddenly fall off after each appreciation—for example, capital equipment for which contracts have been made years in advance. On your second question, I fully agree with you that
German economic policy in recent months has been rather con-
tractionary, so that the unemployment rate is now about 4 percent—the highest it has been since the war. This quite obviously
serves to reduce demand at home, and encourages companies
to expand their exports.

DE CECCO: I have two comments on the German economic
performance. My first remark is that Germany has consistently
refused in the last fifteen years to assume the burden of a reserve currency. My second comment is the usual Italian observation about foreign workers in Germany. When Italians talk
about Germany and its economic miracles, they are inclined to
wonder about the three million workers which Germany can hire
and fire at will. Germany has them as workers; it doesn't have
them as people. The turnover is high, the workers can be used
in their prime, and they can be sent home when no longer wanted.
Now this has not been true of England; the foreign workers come
in, but they don't go out. They are treated as English people.
I would guess that Germany is a unique case in this aspect of
its labor supply.

JAMISON: Professor Sohmen has not stressed three factors
which seem important to me in explaining the high performance
of the German economy—namely, the technological and scien-
tific prowess of West Germany, the stock of modern efficient
capital goods that West Germany has, and the high fraction of

the German gross national product devoted to capital investment that has been evident for many years. Perhaps he would
care to comment on these matters.

SILK: Just a few comments. I don't mean at all to depre-
cate Germany's performance, which has been most impressive.
Professor Sohmen very kindly casts his comparisons in terms
of Germany versus Britain, but there were one or two remarks
about the United States that I feel a need to respond to.

First of all, Egon couldn't pick a worse example of American competitiveness than the steel industry. But there is nothing new in that. During the interwar years, it was like pulling
teeth to get the steel industry to increase capacity, and that is
what our rearmament effort focused on at the beginning of World
War II. In the postwar years, the pattern has been the same;
the steel industry has responded to increases in demand by increasing prices rather than by increasing capacity. If the example set by steel had been followed by other industries, the
United States would have probably performed even less well
than Britain since the war. Fortunately, in some other areas—
including computers, aviation, and agriculture—we did very
well and, until the recent unpleasantness, our trade position
hasn't been bad.

Another factor that has played a part both in Germany's
strength and in America's weakness has been the role of U.S.
capital internationally. Now if we want to think like the labor
unions, we could assume that there was some sort of plot here—
that American industry hated America and just wanted to seek
its fortune abroad. But of course many factors have been involved, including the relative cheapness of European resources
in terms of an overvalued dollar and the desire of U.S. producers to gain, rather than lose, from European trade restrictions.

As for the overall competitiveness of Germany in relation
to the United States, I don't know. I agree that concentration
ratios don't tell us very much, but I think that, on the whole,
our system is still remarkably competitive rather than uncom-
petitive. And this, I think, is really a matter of business behavior rather than mainly a result of antitrust laws.

SCITOVSKY: I am wondering whether Art Laffer's wedge
is a factor in explaining Germany's remarkable economic performance. I get the impression that national defense counts
in much the same way as welfare payments in the wedge, and
it occurs to me that the lower scale of government expenditures

in Germany might be of considerable significance in what we
are trying to explain.

FLEMING: I think that most of the causes of Germany's
great achievements are sociological, but I would like to get
Professor Sohmen's reaction to one or two possible economic
factors. One is the earlier large expansion of the labor force,
drawn from agriculture and from East Germany, which made
it possible to supply the labor that could be combined with the
new efficient capital equipment. The other is the high level of
savings, which I think might be attributed to the fact that the
German population has been accustomed to high taxation from
the time of the Great Depression, then from the Nazi period,
and then from the early postwar period of military control.
At the same time, the ratio of profits to labor cost has been
high; this has also encouraged a great deal of private saving.
And of course one should add Professor Scitovsky's point about
defense expenditures.

I would still adhere to the view, however, that the basic explanation for the German economic performance is probably
sociological. What I have in mind, first of all, is a fear of
inflation coming down from the past—particularly from the
hyperinflation of the 1920s. Among other things, this fear has
probably made workers a bit more modest in their wage claims.
Secondly, the reaction to defeat and impoverishment put Germany on its mettle to achieve the determination necessary to
overcome the difficulties. Thirdly, there was the German willingness to accept Americanism—or what was thought to be
Americanism—a willingness also evident in Japan, and one of
the reasons why Japan went ahead. Fourthly, there has been
the absence of what one might call the "gentleman tradition,"
which has been the bane of British capitalism.

Chairman THORP: Egon, we are not going to have time for
you to comment on all the matters raised, but I will give you
an opportunity to reply to what you regard as the more important points made by other members in this discussion.

SOHMEN: Well, as you indicate, Mr. Chairman, I can't
possibly comment exhaustively on all the questions raised.
Many of the points that have been made I fully agree with, but
it still would seem to me that the competition policy of West
Germany has been a unique feature which I do not really find
in any other country. I am inclined to believe that this policy
has been a major factor in explaining the performance of the
German economy. I'm not thinking just of antitrust policy as

such but of some of the sociological factors mentioned by Marcus Fleming. For example, the inflow of refugees from the east certainly was important—the availability of cheap labor, of people who really wanted to work very hard because they had to. This obviously strengthened the competitive pressure on the rest of the economy even if there had not been a stiff enforcement of the antitrust laws.

I would agree that American aid played a major role in the rebuilding of the German economy. But other countries also received American aid. Britain, for example, received about the same level of aid as Germany, but the results have been very different.

I would agree with Professor Scitovsky that the comparatively low level of military expenditure has made possible a higher rate of capital investment than the American economy has had. Certainly, this is one of the reasons for the difference in growth rates; Germany did not have to fight a war either in Vietnam or, earlier, in Korea. But I would point also to the underutilization of resources in the American economy, where the postwar record has been strikingly from that of Germany. I would guess that this factor has probably resulted in a greater drain in real terms than even these two wars. But it is very difficult to judge that.

VI. STAGFLATION AND THE PRICE OF OIL

Isaiah Frank and
Conference Members

Chairman THORP: Our topic this afternoon is the problem
created by the OPEC countries—a problem that has caused
major strains in the international monetary system and, at
least in the minds of some people, a disastrous situation. As
we talk about this matter, we should bear in mind that many
people are concerned with this state of affairs, not only as an
OPEC problem, but also as a demonstration of possible scarci-
ties and shortages either artificially or naturally created as
the world economy continues to grow. At a recent meeting I
attended in Washington, I felt that some participants were almost hysterical in concluding that all our international economic
policies should be rewritten to make sure that we have appropriate powers, whatever they may be, to deal with the situation—that we should start by trying to establish international
rules about the obligation of countries to export (including soy-
beans, I suppose) and that the Administration should be prepared to use all possible forms of pressure, restriction, and
retaliation in order to deal with these potential future threats.
These were very reasonable and honorable people, some of
them quite high in the business community, and there is little
doubt that this problem will get a good deal of attention. It is
the kind of problem that will attract Congress, because it pro-
vides ammunition for those who are interested in justifying
increased protectionism.

I have asked Isaiah Frank, who has been active in looking
at these matters, to begin the discussion.

ISAIAH FRANK: Let me first raise the narrower issues relating to petroleum and then turn to some of the broader matters raised by the Chairman. I take it that the important facts relating to the oil problem are two: first, the quintupling of the oil price and, second, the selective embargo which exposed the vulnerability of the oil-consuming countries to supply interruptions.

These two facts raise three sets of problems. The first is the problem to which Bob Solomon referred yesterday—how, in the short run or in the medium run, the world accommodates to the international economic and financial consequences of the OPEC actions. The second issue is how, over the longer run, we achieve sufficient independence of the OPEC countries to avoid being vulnerable to the supply and price manipulations of a small group. This second issue involves such questions as emergency sharing, stockpiling, conservation, reserve capacity, and alternative sources of energy. The third set of questions has been raised by the Chairman: To what extent are producers likely to organize cartels for other commodities? What is the prospective scarcity situation in other commodities? What sort of new rules of the game are appropriate?

First, a word about the short-run financial consequences. In rough balance-of-payments terms, the OECD countries have shifted from a current-account surplus of about $12 billion, corresponding roughly to the flow of aid to the less developed countries, to a collective deficit of perhaps $30 billion. At the same time, there has been a massive increase in the current-account deficit of the developing countries amounting possibly to another $30 billion. The counterpart of these deficits, of course, is the current-account surplus of the OPEC countries, amounting in 1974 to roughly $60 billion.

The question that arises from all this is a question, not of policy, but of projection, and that is: what is the likely course of this OPEC surplus over the next few years—say to 1980? Anyone who has followed the subject is bound to be confused, because a variety of different projections have been issued from the same international bodies. The OECD originally had an estimate of $250-325 billion by 1980 in constant dollars; that estimate was later revised downward. The World Bank initially came out with much larger figures; these were also revised downward. The Morgan Guaranty Trust Company has come out with a scenario indicating a cumulative figure by 1978 of about $250 billion in current dollars. For purposes of this discussion, I would be prepared to accept what seems to be a convergence of view between the U. S. Treasury and the OECD of about $200-250 billion by 1980 in constant 1974 dollars, which in current dollars might amount to somewhere between $350 billion and $420 billion.

Whatever the prospects for the OPEC surplus, there are a number of issues requiring examination. The key operational issue is how to recycle the OPEC surplus in such a way that the oil-consuming countries which need funds get them, since there is no necessary correspondence between the distribution of OPEC investments and the distribution of the collective current-account deficit. Now in 1974, to a remarkable extent, private markets managed to achieve such recycling. Toward the end of the year, the situation became more difficult, and it is unlikely that private markets can solve the recycling problem by themselves. As a result, new arrangements are being established—arrangements which inevitably have raised new questions. One of the hesitations that the United States has had with respect to the IMF oil facility is that it is a nice cozy arrangement for the OPEC, all risk being collectively assumed by the oil-importing countries. The OPEC gets gilt-edged paper completely protected from what might be a very healthy kind of fear—namely, the fear of the possibility of freezing or sterilizing of OPEC assets in case of another oil embargo. Other arrangements include the proposed so-called "third window" of the World Bank, which may well turn out to be a very constructive innovation as a method of conveying aid to the developing countries.

Another issue—perhaps it is not an issue, but many people believe it is—is whether, as OPEC countries shift from short-term assets and bank deposits to longer-term investments, we ought to be worried about problems of control and of the political consequences of control. For the first time, many people in the United States are beginning to react the way people abroad—both in the developing countries and in Western Europe—have reacted who have been on the receiving end of large-scale American direct investment. Here the suggestions range from provisions for assembling information to screening provisions requiring prenotification in cases where equity investment would exceed 5 percent of the total (and thus presumably imply foreign control).

Let me now turn to the effect of the OPEC price increases on producers and consumers of other commodities. Producers

of other primary products may, of course, be inspired to do
the same thing. At the same time, there has been an impact
on the consuming countries. A number of people, including
people of the American government, appear more willing at
the moment to look sympathetically at efforts to create international arrangements for particular commodities which might
serve to stabilize producer incomes and to do so at acceptable
levels. This is a consequence, I think, not only of the OPEC
actions but also of the very sharp upward movement in many
commodity prices since 1972. One question very much in the
picture is the issue of "indexation," which Lord Robbins raised
in a domestic context. At the international level, we find a
clamor for indexation, not only with respect to oil prices, for
which the Shah of Iran has been a principal proponent, but also
with respect to an UNCTAD list of eighteen basic commodities
under a system of simultaneously negotiated commodity agreements.

On another matter, the Chairman has raised the question of
whether we should attempt to elaborate rules dealing with access to supplies as a companion to rules relating to access to
markets. Here people may have various types of restriction
in mind. One form of supply restriction has been in response
to fears of inflation; the soybean example mentioned by the
Chairman was of this type. Other supply restrictions have as
their purpose the raising of prices; the OPEC case is a clear
example of that. Then there are supply restrictions adopted
for so-called "national security" reasons. Here the United
States is doubtless as guilty as others with its so-called "stra-
tegic trade controls." In this area, thinking runs largely in
terms of the need for prior international consultation, for rules
to protect importing countries, and for rules to assure that
supply restrictions are eliminated as soon as they ought to be.
One country which has scarcely been mentioned thus far—
namely, Japan—has an intense interest in this matter, and I
think there would be a collective interest in doing something
about it.

In looking at this whole business of producer controls and
producer cartels, I am wondering whether we shouldn't dust
off the old international trade agreement which was buried
twenty-five years ago, shortly after it was negotiated, and take
another look at those chapters dealing with international cartels and commodity agreements. One of the contentions of the
developing countries is that they would not be very receptive

to restraints on the right to enter into producer cartels involving primary commodities unless comparable restraints were
placed on obstacles to competition in manufactured goods. This
brings us back to the chapter in the ITO charter dealing with
restrictive practices, both public and private.

So, Mr. Chairman, the range of issues is very wide. I myself don't think that scarcity is the main issue; to the extent
that careful projections have been made, they indicate that we
can expect lower relative prices for most primary commodities, say in the period 1980-85, than we have had in the last
few years. But I have said enough for the time being.

Chairman THORP: Are there any comments on this rather
overwhelming presentation? Professor Douglass:

DOUGLASS: While others are collecting their thoughts on
more important issues, let me say a word about the future
price of oil. It would appear that the large integrated energy
companies are studying this matter rather carefully at the
present time. There have been recent news reports of a number of withdrawals of participation in projects involving major
investments in alternative energy sources. The reason appears
to be the expectation of a significant break in the price of oil
that would make such investments unprofitable. This suggests
that we can look forward to a price for oil much nearer to real
costs for the next few years and, by the time the world starts
looking like a Swiss cheese, perhaps a considerably lower price
starting in the early 1980s.

SCHMIDT: I think it is rather important how one thinks
about this problem of the oil-price increase. In balance-of-
payments terms, if one is a Keynesian, one cares about the
current account; if one is a monetarist under a system of fixed
exchange rates, one cares about the overall balance—in technical terms, the "official reserve transactions" balance. The
Keynesian views the impact of the oil crisis as an unfavorable
change in relative prices—very unfavorable in the case of the
United States; in fact, it took something like 17 percent of the
rise in the nominal GNP out of the country. But if one is a
monetarist, the oil-price rise has had very little impact in
terms of aggregate demand levels because exchange rates are
floating. In fact, if I can figure out the numbers correctly, the
higher oil price and its repercussions have washed out in the
U.S. balance of payments, with little if any impact on exchange
rates or on reserves. Now whether one is a Keynesian or a
monetarist does have a very important effect on how serious

one thinks the problem is. If one is a monetarist, and if currencies are floating, one will tend to think that the problem is small. A monetarist would say that there is only one real impact—namely, the adverse effect on the terms of trade. Well, the thing that has to be remembered there is that, not only did the price of oil go up, but also the prices of U.S. exports and, in fact, the prices of exports of all industrial countries. Between October 1973 and October 1974, the terms-of-trade cost for the industrial countries was only about 1.4 percent of real GNP, or something like that; the figure for the United States was 1.5 percent. If one is a Keynesian, this may seem like a costly operation. If one is a monetarist, all that has happened is that the ownership of some of the U.S. money supply has shifted from Americans to Middle Easterners or Western Europeans. In other words, the foreign component of the U.S. money stock has risen, as it has been rising very substantially in the last two or three years.

One final matter. I would like Isaiah Frank to comment on the concept of a floor price for oil; I don't understand the strategy of the U.S. government in seeking a floor price.

WHITMAN: I thought that Wilson Schmidt's discussion of the difference between the Keynesian and the monetarist view was important, but there is one thing that is missed in both the Keynesian and the monetarist analysis of this situation, and that is the very substantial structural wrench which is given to any economy by a sharp and sudden shift in relative prices. Such a shift is bound to worsen the short-run relationship between inflation and unemployment. This applies both to the increase in relative prices brought about by the OPEC countries and to any further increase in relative prices if we were to impose a tariff on oil; the latter action, in the short run, inevitably would make the structural wrench worse. I can't think of any macroeconomic policy or any sleight of hand that would dispose of this problem.

SOLOMON: Just two comments, one in reaction to Wilson Schmidt and the other on how one thinks about this problem. If I understand Wilson correctly, his conclusion about the cost being 1.5 percent of GNP was arrived at by monetarist reasoning. It so happens that if one looks at the matter in Keynesian terms, the current-account deficit of the OECD countries also amounts to roughly 1.5 percent of the OECD gross national product. So, Wilson, you have the same burden whichever route you use. Whether you want to make light of 1.5 percent

of GNP is not clear to me. I don't know how much importance
to attach to the real burden of the oil-price rise, but I would
not dismiss it quite as cavalierly as you seem to do.

My second point is that political and economic questions
tend to get all mixed up in this matter, and it is hard to have
a coherent discussion unless the parties are agreed on whether
they are discussing politics or economics. We can talk about
the economics of the higher oil price, which involves financing
problems, transfer problems, and income-burden problems,
or we can discuss political questions involving the rise of the
new group of powerful oil-producing nations, whose wealth will
accumulate, as Isaiah Frank has told us, to somewhere between
$250 billion and $400 billion. Whether we are mainly concerned
with economic questions or with political questions will have a
great deal to do with the sort of prescriptions we put forward.

GRASSMAN: One point in Professor Frank's survey deserves
more attention. He implied, without giving any reasons, that
the problems of financial adjustment stemming from the oil-
price rise will be even greater in the future than they have been
thus far. We could, I think, make the opposite argument that
the worst is over and that, on the whole, the market has settled
this shock surprisingly well. I would be very interested in any
evidence or arguments about why adjustment problems in this
area should become more difficult as time goes on. Professor
McKinnon yesterday referred to one possible difficulty—the lack
of stabilizing speculation in the exchange market and the reluc-
tance of banks to take open positions. In Europe, this situation
is mainly due, I think, to central bank restrictions; in the United
States, it may be due to purely commercial or prudential considerations, but it does seem to be a fact. This is a problem, of
course, but I see no reason why it should become worse, now
that all of the major agents in the financial markets have, to a
large extent, learned the new game.

SILK: Just a word about Wilson Schmidt's figure of 1.5 percent. Surely that figure has to be too low as a measure of the
burden. For one thing, it is related only to oil. The prices
of competitive fuels have also risen dramatically in recent
months; for example, coal prices have more than tripled. The
price of natural gas has not risen that much because of control,
but it has risen substantially. In any case, there has been a
strong upward push to the overall cost structure.

Let me conclude with a word about the longer-run question
of scarcity, to which Isaiah Frank referred. I certainly agree

that in the short run we did not run out of oil and that the major cause of the rise in the price was cartel behavior, so the Club of Rome gets no credit for that. At the same time, unless we treat the OPEC statements about wasting assets as sheer propaganda or meaningless rhetoric—which I don't—then we do have cause for concern about the future.

WILLETT: I think that Marina Whitman made a useful qualification to what Wilson Schmidt was saying about the difference between the monetarists and the Keynesians. She argued, I think rightly, that the oil-price increase was bound to worsen the inflation-unemployment trade-off. I agree with Leonard Silk that this worsening is understated if we simply make a calculation of the effect of the oil-price increase by itself, without taking into account all of the induced effects. I also agree with Bob Solomon that 1.5 percent or 2 percent of GNP is not small by any means. The German reparation problem after World War I was, as Fritz Machlup has shown, a matter of 2 percent of GNP, but this does not mean that the problem was trivial.

ALIBER: Having been trained at Yale and having taught at the University of Chicago, I think I can speak with authority on the Keynesians and the monetarists. It seems to me that the two groups ought to agree that adjustment to the higher oil price cannot be rapid, and may be painful. For one thing, millions of people have to be shifted out of existing jobs into other occupations. This is a painful business, whichever label you wear.

WALLICH: We all seem to be expressing somewhat similar ideas in different analytical contexts. I would respond to Wilson Schmidt by saying that the monetarists would hold that aggregate demand in nominal terms has remained unchanged if the supply of money has remained unchanged. But if the price level rises as a result of a higher price for oil, then real income falls. And if money wages rise as a result of a higher cost of living, then unemployment will also rise. So constant aggregate demand doesn't help us very much; under such conditions, the monetarists arrive at the same conclusions as the Keynesians.

On the question of the painfulness of the oil-price rise, a country can completely postpone the real cost of larger oil payments if it borrows this amount from abroad—that is to say, if it has a current-account deficit equal to the increase in its oil payments. Whether it will have such a deficit will depend very largely on international capital movements. Assuming that market forces are allowed to have their way and that the

OPEC countries invest in the oil-importing countries, then the current account of the oil-importing countries can be in deficit, with little if any change in exchange rates. If such investment does not take place, the oil-importing countries will be forced into current-account balance at lower exchange rates. In this case, the real burden will be immediate.

One final twist. It may not make a great deal of difference whether the OPEC countries invest in the oil-importing countries, so long as they invest abroad. If capital markets are efficient, capital can flow into the oil-importing countries from investment sources in third countries that are importing capital from OPEC countries. So one comes to the conclusion that whether there is a real burden in the short run depends on whether a country is forced into current-account balance at a lower exchange rate or is permitted to develop a current-account deficit financed by capital imports.

Chairman THORP: While we are on the subject of capital movements, I hope that someone will explain how one avoids the sudden withdrawal of the enormous short-term deposits held abroad by the oil-producing countries. This is at least an immediate problem and one that may prove very difficult to deal with. Frank Tamagna has something to say on this matter.

TAMAGNA: The Arabs are already moving into medium-term foreign investment, and we may expect that they will be moving into the bond and stock market, particularly because the stock market is now going up. Now what would be the disadvantage if, say, half of Arab oil revenues were to be placed in direct investments abroad? I think that politically it would be very good, because it would give us a hostage in case there were any action that we might want to take politically or economically. If Arab revenues are recycled via long-term or direct investment, the payments naturally would be spread over a longer period of time. Thus the current-account position would not react as quickly as if the oil revenues were used for imports, but I am wondering why we should always think in terms of the current account and the short-term capital account instead of thinking in terms of adjustment by long-term or direct investment. I wonder whether Isaiah Frank would like to comment on this.

FRANK: I don't think that this is a question of our thinking; it's a question of how the OPEC thinks—of how the OPEC wants to dispose of its payments surpluses.

TAMAGNA: Well, as I said, the Arabs are moving into medium-term investment, and they are probably already moving into the longer-term account. Some countries, including the United States, have taken a hard-line attitude about such long-term investment. I think it would be wiser for us to be more liberal in this respect. Of course, it is not a question of either-or. I don't want to give the impression that adjustment should be exclusively via long-term investment. What I can visualize is a mixture of various forms of recycling involving both the current and the capital account.

FRANK: I have no quarrel with that perspective.

Chairman THORP: Isaiah Frank referred to the fact that there are people who are worried about the United States becoming owned by the Arabs, and there is a threat of legislation which would prevent the Arabs, the Japanese, and other foreigners from investing in this country. Of course this will create a big battle in Washington, because Americans interested in investing abroad will fear backlashes all over the place if we stop foreigners from investing in this country. Moreover, our investment abroad is much greater than the investment by foreigners in the United States. Incidentally, if you were impressed by the amount of foreign investment in the United States last year, bear in mind that a very large part of that is accounted for by the Arab purchase of Aramco. It is a little hard for me to visualize the kind of threat that people see in foreign investment in the United States when this merely takes the form of foreigners taking over the operation, in their own countries, of American companies.

TAMAGNA: May I also point out that, since the period for which we expect the deficit is comparatively short, the amount of OPEC investment in the United States would be small as compared with U. S. investment abroad. Assuming that less than half of OPEC direct investment would be in this country, it would hardly be a significant factor in the U. S. economy.

ALIBER: When you speak of direct investment, Frank, what do you have in mind?

TAMAGNA: Buying U. S. Steel.

ALIBER: Buying shares of U. S. Steel?

TAMAGNA: Yes, I mean stock in U. S. Steel—stock investment.

Chairman THORP: Of course, direct investment also includes such things as, for instance, the Japanese purchase of hotels in Hawaii. Included, too, would be the investment by foreigners in land development that is taking place in some sections of the United States.

TAMAGNA: An example is a recent report of Kuwait buying real estate on the Atlantic coast.

FLEMING: I agree strongly with Mr. Tamagna's point; in fact, I'd like to carry it a bit further. As international economists, I think we really ought to feel sad at the speed with which the current-account disequilibrium is being rectified, because it means that 1.5 percent of world real income is being wasted on armaments and on hasty investment that is almost bound to be uneconomic. One good aspect of OPEC policy was to create a great new source of savings in the world which could have been useful if properly distributed. But people became so worried about the current-account deficits that they rejoice when they see them go down. I quite agree with Mr. Tamagna that it would be much better if the Arabs were to invest all over the industrial world as well as the less developed world, spreading their funds as thinly as possible but nevertheless holding them in places where they would be most productive. And, on another matter, I think it's a great mistake to feel that one is threatened because other people have investments in one's country. In the old days, it was the creditor who had the gunboats, but when the debtor has the gunboats there is really no cause for fear.

TRIFFIN: In speaking of Arab investments, I would like to stress that there are three types. The first is short-term, highly volatile liquid claims. Borrowing countries don't like hot money of this kind, because it may move suddenly from one country to another, creating exchange crises. The lenders don't like it very much either, because of the possibility of politically motivated blocking. They are very aware that, in the case of another war with Israel, the U. S. Treasury might block such claims; indeed, such considerations had much to do with the origin of the Eurodollar market, where the Russians had the same concern.

DE CECCO: A good example was in 1957, when the United States placed an embargo on the funds of Middle Eastern countries that participated in the Suez conflict.

TRIFFIN: Exactly. As far as long-term investment is concerned, the borrowing countries don't like it very much because they are worried, rightly or wrongly, about the control of their enterprises by foreigners. But the Arabs don't like it either, because they are well aware that if they acquire too much, it will be expropriated and nationalized, as has often happened in the past. There is a third type of investment which is beginning to emerge, and that is advance payments on long-term contracts. It seems to me that transactions of this kind should have priority as a means of solving the recycling problem.

TAMAGNA: Such advance payments may be subject to the same risks as other forms of investment. If, for example, there is a seven-year contract for delivery of equipment to Saudi Arabia and, in the meantime, there is an Israeli war, the delivery could be suspended.

TRIFFIN: I would add that part of the explanation for the weakness of the dollar may be the fear, justified by past experience, that the United States under such conditions might block funds or place controls on U. S. exports.

JAMISON: Earlier, Mr. Tamagna used the term "hostage." With this idea in mind, it seems to me that, from a Machiavellian perspective of power politics and national self-interest, it might be to our advantage to have a substantial Arab investment in the United States.

Chairman THORP: Arthur Young is a man who at a very early stage helped Saudi Arabia to modernize its finances. I would be interested to know if he has anything to say about this problem.

ARTHUR N. YOUNG: First, let me say that Isaiah Frank described the situation very effectively, and I concur in his analysis. I might stress two or three points that have occurred to me. One rather obvious point is that investing within the OPEC countries is going to absorb a fair amount of the increase in oil revenues. For example, there are projects in Saudi Arabia involving agreements with Aramco for using natural gas. If you fly over that area, you see gas flaring out of tall chimneys all over the country. Instead of wasting it, the Saudi Arabians would like to use the gas effectively to develop a steel industry. They don't have the iron ore, of course, but the same observation applies to Japan and other countries. They also want to develop in other sectors, so there should be a continuing demand for capital goods and other products which will absorb more of the oil revenues than some of the pessimists originally believed. Of course, it is to be hoped that not too much will go into armament.

The surplus really concentrates on Saudi Arabia, which has far and away the largest oil deposits of any country. Kuwait and the emirates along the coast are also very rich. These areas have small populations, with huge increases in per capita wealth, if you care to figure it that way—which may not be a very satisfactory way to figure it.

A long-run problem that worries me relates to the piling up of debt in this recycling process—first in such countries as Britain and Italy but above all else in the non-OPEC developing countries. In those countries, we know that the burden of debt had been increasing at an alarming rate long before the oil embargo. It probably more than doubled in the five years before the embargo, with the debt service reaching $5-7 billion a year. And that may be expected to increase hugely.

I've had some experience in these matters, and it seems to me that the debts of some of these developing countries will become so large that we will have to make a series of settlements— first stretching out the principal over a longer period of time and then, perhaps, reducing the interest. Of course, since some of these debts are fixed in certain currencies, inflation may tend to ease the burden.

Chairman THORP: For a number of countries, we have already been faced with the necessity of renegotiating debts. The main procedure is to take the overdue debt, plus perhaps the debt for the next year or two, and place it at the end of whatever series of future payments is in effect. The net result, of course, is that the total debt burden is extended into the future. While this relieves the pressure at the moment, it doesn't assure that in the long run the pressure is going to be relieved.

FRANK: Just a short footnote, Mr. Chairman, on Arthur Young's interesting remark on debt. Whether or not inflation eases the debt burden of the developing countries depends very much on what happens to their terms of trade. If inflation is accompanied by a deterioration in their terms of trade—if prices of their imports of manufactured goods go up more rapidly than the prices of their exports of primary products—then they could be worse off than they would have been in the absence of inflation.

ARTHUR N. YOUNG: I would agree with that as a possibility, of course. The effect of inflation will vary in each particular situation, but I think the long-term trend would be to ease the debt burden of the developing countries—though by no means equally.

SOLOMON: Marcus Fleming said earlier that it would be very nice if we were not so anxious to remove quickly the

current-account deficit of the oil-importing countries. He
would like to see adjustment taking place over a longer period
with the help of capital movements. I would simply like to point
out that some of the oil-importing countries have credit problems—or at least the market thinks they do—so that there is
concern among such countries about accumulating debt over a
lengthy period. Some of them would prefer to make the real
transfer earlier rather than later just to avoid that problem.
In any event, it is not up to us oil importers how fast the OPEC
surplus is going to disappear; it depends on the rapidity with
which OPEC countries increase their imports.

TAMAGNA: Or their investments.

SOLOMON: Well, I'm talking about the current-account
surplus, and how quickly that disappears depends upon three
variables. The first is what happens to the price of oil. The
second is what happens to the rate of growth of OPEC imports.
The third is what happens to the demand curve for petroleum
in the oil-importing countries as a result of conservation efforts
and substitution efforts.

SCHMIDT: The fourth is what happens to the price of imports.

SILK: The fifth is what happens to salesmanship, especially
at the Pentagon.

SOLOMON: I accept those addenda. My next point is that
when one observes the ambitious investment programs that are
being planned in the OPEC countries, I think one is forced to
the conclusion that there is likely to be severe inflation in some
of those countries. I would liken the situation to what happened
in Spain when gold poured in during the sixteenth century.

TAMAGNA: And silver.

SOLOMON: Gold and silver. In any event, I suspect there
will be rather severe inflation in the OPEC area, and I don't
know whether anyone has thought through what the implications
are. The reason I predict inflation is that, while the OPEC
countries can have ambitious investment programs, they can't
import everything; some local resources are necessarily uti-
lized. Labor is limited and, for social reasons, a number of
these countries do not want to import labor because they don't
want to change the nature of their societies.

My final point is in response to the hope of the Chairman
that someone will say something about hot money. I'm not
sure that I will make him sleep any better, but it seems to me
that one ray of hope is that, as the OPEC countries acquire a

large stake in any given financial asset or in any given currency, to some degree they become locked in, because any effort
to get out will drive down the price of what they have, and this
will serve as a deterrent to large-scale shifting around of OPEC
hot money. In other words, the money may not be as hot as it
appears.

SILK: Just to repeat: my point five on Bob Solomon's list
is not to forget salesmanship, especially at the Pentagon, as
a factor in wiping out the OPEC current-account surplus. And
it isn't only the Pentagon, of course, but also the French, the
German, and other defense establishments. Armament is pouring into the OPEC area, and that is a very dangerous development. Such expenditure largely accounts, I think, for the greater
than anticipated rise in OPEC imports.

I would like to add to Bob Solomon's Spanish point, since I
was a student of Earl Hamilton in the days when he was at Duke.
What Professor Hamilton's research showed was that the trea-
sure flowing to Spain did not stay there but found its way north,
where it financed the Industrial Revolution in Britain, France,
and elsewhere in northern Europe.

Well, if history has any relevance to the present situation,
there may be extremely interesting international flows of funds.
On the basis of what has happened thus far, I suppose we would
have to say that the United States is not the Britain of the new
Industrial Revolution. The prime candidate ought to be Germany. I think that a good deal of the German strength—Professor Sohmen may correct me on this point—has been related
in this recent period to the flow of money out of the Middle East
in exchange for German goods, both military and civilian.

LAFFER: It seems to me that the present situation is very
different from the one studied by Earl Hamilton, in which the
world was rather suddenly confronted with a sharp autonomous
increase in the supply of monetary assets. In the case of the
OPEC countries, we have a huge increase in the demand for
reserves, which has actually caused much of the increase in
the supply of reserves. And the results in terms of inflation
are quite different from what they would be if this increase in
demand were not present. This is the only point I'd like to
make in this connection, but it means that the inflationary impact of the increase in reserves may be less serious than many
people fear.

SCHMIDT: I don't want to let the record rest with Bob Solomon's statement that I was somehow being cavalier about the

real cost of the oil-price increase. My key point is that I am
actually very worried about the costs that we may inflict upon
ourselves by our response to the OPEC challenge. Dr. Kissinger has used the figure of a capital investment of $500 billion
as our response. How he came to this estimate, and over what
length of time, I don't know. But it seems to me absolutely
essential to be right on our policy in this matter, because extra-
ordinary amounts of resources can be wasted by governments
in trying to deal with what may be a fairly modest issue.

FRANK: I would like to ask Wilson what he means by a waste
of resources. If he is talking about economic waste in the sense
that we are going to be developing resources which ought to be
available more cheaply elsewhere, that is one thing that I understand. But I take it that a big component of the $500 billion is
national-security expenditures. If Wilson views national-security
expenditures as a waste of resources, again I can understand
what he is saying, but the burden of the argument for these big
expenditures on alternative energy supplies rests on national-
security grounds.

SCHMIDT: May I try to explain what I meant. Bob Aliber
had an article in the Wall Street Journal this week which suggests that there is a good deal of chipping away at the oil price.
Now if, after agreeing on a floor price, we find ourselves moving back toward relatively low-priced oil, we are going to have
an entirely unwarranted rate of implicit effective protection of
petroleum and related industries in the OECD area that will
cost us for the rest of our lives. What I'm saying is that the
real problem is not the OPEC monopoly but our possible response to it, which could involve extremely inefficient and
wasteful use of scarce resources.

TRIFFIN: If I may add to what Wilson has said, I agree
fully that the floor price for oil that is envisaged will be very
costly in the long run. Politically, I see in it the seed of major
confrontation later on with the Europeans arising from our
efforts to protect our competitiveness by asking them to impose
the same high price on their citizens, even though much of the
development may be in our country. I think that this will be
a serious political issue before long.

I also share Wilson's concern about the $500 billion or more
that we propose to spend in the next few years, the results of
which, in terms of consumable output, will come only much
later. In the meantime, we will be building up an enormous
inflationary potential. And we should think very carefully about

the military implications.   The high floor price for oil is essentially a military consideration, and the buildup of armaments in
the Middle East not only is a waste of resources, but adds to a
powder keg which will make a mockery of the estimates and fore-
casts that we have been brandishing around this table.   Militarily,
this may all be justified, but I would not simply take the word of
the Pentagon for it.

DE CECCO: I agree completely with the last statement of
Professor Triffin.   Regarding the possibility of a clash between
the United States and Europe on the floor price, let me first re-
fer to a point of fact: the American suggestion is $7 a barrel;
the European suggestion is $6.

HABERLER: Oh, no; it is more than that.

DE CECCO: No, it is $6.   This is the latest figure; I heard
the news in Paris the day before coming here.   In fact, one of
the European fears is that the difference is only $1.   But the
matter is complicated, because the issue is really the price of
energy rather than the price of oil.   The Europeans have a big
stake in nuclear programs, at least on paper, and those things
are rather expensive.   Also, North Sea oil doesn't make much
sense at a price below $6, though Lord Robbins is much better
qualified than I am to comment on that.   At any rate, it used to
be the producers of oil against everybody else; now it's the producers of energy against everybody else.

FRANK: For the purpose of clarifying the discussion, I think
one needs to differentiate two issues.   One issue is whether or
not the West should attempt to achieve a certain degree of independence from OPEC supply.   The floor price is an entirely
separate issue; it is simply a technique for guaranteeing a reasonable return on American and other investments in higher-
priced oil.   I myself think that this is a crazy way of doing it,
since there are better alternatives.   To have a floor price—
especially a common floor price—seems to make no sense at
all.   But the two issues are completely separate.

WILLETT: I agree with the general thrust of Professor
De Cecco's comments on the convergence of American and European views, but I don't want to let the record stand that the
United States has proposed a floor price of $7.   The U. S. gov-
ernment has not yet made any official proposal regarding the
oil-price level, and there has been considerable disagreement
within the government both on whether the floor price is a desirable technique and, if it is, on what the price should be.   I
guess that it is no secret that the State Department and the

Treasury Department have somewhat different views about the technical means of achieving their common objectives.

Chairman THORP: You're making a general statement, I assume—not one just related to this problem.

WILLETT: No comment!

Lord ROBBINS: Whatever the views of the State Department and the Treasury Department, the floor price is passionately supported by the Scottish nationalists.

SILK: Could I ask Tom Willett if he would clarify for us which agency of the U. S. government—Treasury or State—is on top with respect to this floor-price matter? Would he also interpret the recent news from the International Energy Agency to the effect that eighteen countries have agreed to establish something like a floor price?

WILLETT: I won't comment on your first question except to say that we each have our own views on the ups and downs of State and Treasury. On your second question, there is still a great deal of disagreement on technique, but I think it is fair to say that there is rather general agreement on the idea of giving some price protection to a wide range of energy suppliers. There also is fairly general agreement that this should not be achieved at anything close to the present level of $10-11 per barrel. In other words, the price should be well above the old price of oil and well below the present price.

FRANK: Is the implication of what you have said, Tom, that there is international agreement on the concept of a floor price?

WILLETT: The answer, I think, is yes, although one can get into semantic questions about exactly what is meant by a floor price. Official statements from the International Energy Agency do not use the term floor price, but the idea is certainly implied. In a broad sense, there seems to be general agreement.

Chairman THORP: Does this include the Arabs?

WILLETT: No, though their pronouncements tend to be in support of the idea—at least the ones I've seen.

DE CECCO: May I add something about the Arabs? Here, I think, one has to distinguish between those who have a lot of oil in the ground and those who don't. This means Saudi Arabia, for example, against Algeria and the Shah. The long-term strategy for a low oil price makes sense for Saudi Arabia; it does not make sense for the Shah, who wants to develop his country in ten years.

SCHMIDT: I would like to pursue the quite useful distinction that Isaiah Frank has made between the national-security issue and the other issues involved in the oil price. If you look at the documentation behind the petroleum import-fee proposal, you will find that the Secretary of the Treasury rested half his case on the balance-of-payments effects of the oil problem. Now, under a regime of floating exchange rates, this doesn't make much sense to me. My second point, relating to national security, is more basic. If you look at Secretary Simon's testimony of January 12, 1975, and do some rough calculations, you will discover that the average price of oil in the United States, after all the taxes that are being proposed, would decline to domestic producers. The inescapable conclusion is that, instead of this being a protectionist program designed to stimulate domestic oil production on national-defense grounds, it is something altogether else. What it is, I don't know, and hence my plea: would somebody please explain to me U. S. government policy in the field of oil?

Chairman THORP: There seems to be a moment of silence.

WHITMAN: Prayerful silence!

SILK: I would be delighted to explain U. S. government policy. Such policy, from one important source in government, had been to establish an $11 price for oil. Congress went into shock over that—as did the rest of the country. So the government is now in the process of negotiating a price below $11 but above what it used to be.

SOLOMON: As a member of an independent agency in the U. S. government, I can only hope that Leonard is wrong.

WALLICH: First, let me say that I hold no brief for the policies that are being discussed. I would like to add to what Wilson Schmidt said a minute ago—not only does the average oil price decline for U. S. producers under current Administration proposals but, even worse, the marginal price declines. In other words, the price of newly found oil—the reward to enterprise for drilling—goes down, and that is a very serious matter.

But let me put this in a broader context. I think we made a great mistake when we took it for granted that the oil cartel would collapse and that nothing was to be done which would interfere with that natural economic process—including no efforts to improve recycling and no efforts to help producers make sure that they weren't going to lose their shirts if they invested in new capacity. Well, we've backed away from that position, and I think we are right in doing something now to encourage producers rather than relying completely on the free market. The risks are very high—particularly when we take into account, not just additional oil, but substitute sources of energy, whether coal, nuclear, thermal, or whatever. But producers do need some assurance.

Now Isaiah Frank has said that there are better ways of providing such assurance than a floor price, and I very much agree with that. In the past, we've had techniques like fast write-offs, for example. The basic principle of what we ought to achieve is very clear: we have to create substitute resources. At the same time, we must put ourselves in a position such that, if the Arabs cut the price, we are not hooked by our substitute sources but can go back to cheap oil. That means protecting the producers who have invested their money, putting the substitute sources in mothballs, and using the cheap oil until the Arabs conceivably turn off the tap again, at which time we would go back to our substitute sources.

There is a story of a wise old monkey who told a chicken to turn itself into a duck. When the chicken asked how to do that, the monkey said, "That's an operating problem; I make policy." I don't know how we accomplish this mothballing of substitute facilities, but I think the general thrust of what we ought to do is clear.

SILK: Just a last word on oil. I think that the record ought to show that not everybody at the conference forgot about conservation. Our whole discussion has proceeded in terms of additional supplies, but, for the intermediate period and probably for the long run as well, conservation deserves fully as much emphasis, if not more.

VII. ISSUES IN THE LONGER RUN

Leonard S. Silk and
Conference Members

Chairman THORP: Several members have suggested that some important considerations may have been overlooked in the process of discussing international economic problems by bits and pieces, and that we ought at some point to take a look at our problems as a whole. This is a little unusual for economists to do. We move from problem to problem rather than contemplating the totality, and it will be rather interesting to see whether we can put the pieces together. Fortunately, we have one member who has to do this quite frequently—Leonard Silk. I have asked him to open the discussion.

LEONARD S. SILK: I take it as my chore this morning to talk briefly on some theoretical problems of the capitalist system as they relate to other kinds of systems that we share on this rather small globe. What are the problems which, if there were time, we would want to discuss? First of all, I think we have to ask, can we solve the problem of inflation, domestically and internationally? Secondly, can we solve the problem of recession or depression? Thirdly, can we solve the problem of economic growth? Do we want to solve that problem any more? This topic was so fashionable as to become almost boring a very few years ago; suddenly, we wonder whether we've been marching in the wrong direction. Fourthly, is it possible to build a more stable world monetary system? This relates at least to the first and second questions, and probably to the third as well. Fifthly, there is, of course, the political-military problem that affects the entire world and that both affects, and is affected by, economic problems.

There is a new problem which economists have, for the most part, treated with a degree of rage that makes me think it is a very real problem—because that's the way the world usually reacts to problems it doesn't want to hear about—and that is the area of depletable resources, pollution, and such matters. These issues are related very closely to the subject of economic growth. But it's simply not the growth question anymore. Before the resources problem came to the forefront, some people—even including Professor Galbraith—raised questions about the desirability of growth in the absence of resource constraints. The basic Galbraith thesis, which was only about 100 percent wrong, was that the problem of scarcity had been solved and that we were capable of growing forever to the point of nausea, but was that really the thing to do? Well, without getting into the over-the-cliff questions posed by the Club of Rome, that conception of the problem has been radically changed, not only by the researches of geologists and ecologists, but also by political events which either correctly, or with a certain degree of distortion, dramatized the problem of scarcity.

Finally, there is the question which Willard suggested would be nice to talk about—namely, what about the state of economics? Do economists have anything to say that is relevant to all these issues or at least to some of them?

On the problem of inflation, obviously economics does have a lot to say. Some of it is a bit contradictory, which leads me to the footnote that economists, more than people in any other field I know of, love to destroy each other. Economics really must be the most contentious of all fields—one in which efforts to find agreement are remarkably rare. There seem to be few brownie points to be earned from moving over to accept a position of an opponent in an economic debate. The name of the game is, destroy the S.O.B.! Forgive my putting it that way, but, having been around quite a while in the field, I think that this is a fair characterization of the normal mode of economic discourse.

Of course there are some matters on which there is more or less general agreement: Money matters. Money is not all that matters. Fiscal policy matters. The institutional structure of society matters. Resources, rates of development, wars, and a host of other factors matter in terms of the

ultimate course of prices. Governmental policies which are
responsive to popular demands tend to resolve conflicts in an
inflationary way in our time, and that is the basic reason why
it is so difficult to deal with the problem of inflation. So we
have faced, and are still facing, the need for some combination
of macroeconomic and microeconomic policies to deal with a
problem that no country has perfectly solved. Some countries
have solved it more successfully than others, and we are still
experimentally groping for answers while listening to sweeping
ideological statements about the end of civilization as we have
known it being nigh if we don't end inflation by next Saturday.

On the problem of depression, I think economists can feel
more confident that they have done well by mankind. Though
some of us assert that we are now in a depression, I think in
fairness it needs to be said that if we mean by that term what
it meant in the 1930s, we would have to say that we are not yet
in a depression. We might call it a mini-depression. I don't
love that terminology, but what we have is more of a mini-depression than a maxi-depression.

Chairman THORP: How about a "maxi-recession"?

SILK: It's a maxi-recession; that we can certainly say, but
it's still in that class—cruiser size rather than dreadnaught
size. But Heaven knows it could get much worse if we did all
the wrong things, and that remains to be seen. Some of the
things we're doing may turn out to be wrong from this standpoint if we are overly obsessed with the problem of inflation.
There are timing problems here that are obviously very difficult. But we do know quite a bit about methods of increasing
demand and employment, and there is something approaching
broad consensus except for a small number of quite old-fashioned
people who believe in equilibrium coming about from wage and
price adjustments if government will just get out of the way.
Except for the annoying fact that this view is shared by the Wall
Street Journal, I don't think it matters.

Now a word about the economic growth problem. I am one
of the pessimists of our time on the growth-resources issue,
because I probably spend more time than most economists do
listening to noneconomists, including scientists of all sorts.
I really do think that economists ought to pay more attention to
other people's data. They have such poor data of their own that
one would think they would go in search of better data but, no,
they like their data; bad as it is, it's theirs. Of course there
are a few exceptions, such as Kenneth Boulding. And there is

a growing group of people who really feel that the growth-resources problem is one that doesn't sit comfortably in the field of conventional economics, which on the whole has been very short-term oriented, but with a long-term faith that if we went on allocating resources on the basis of a more or less static model, everything would all come out right. In such thinking, it seems to me, lies a huge concealed assumption—that though economists like to talk about scarcity, they are not talking about macro-scarcity, or scarcity of the earth's resources; they are talking about particular kinds of scarcity and, hence, of substitutability. I find it very interesting that Bob Solow of all people, a very bright guy, should on this problem tell us exactly what economists have been telling each other on problems that were no different from how a firm allocates resources for the sake of maximizing profits. In a different setting, almost everyone has learned the lesson that one doesn't give micro answers to macro problems. But the growth-resources problem is a macro problem, and one doesn't solve it by substitution any more than one solves aggregate demand and employment problems by substitution.

In order to bring my remarks to a quick close, I'm going to omit the whole question of how to build a better world monetary system, since much of our discussion at this conference has been about that. On the business of the state of the art of economics, I would have to give a pretty low mark these days—perhaps a D+—not because the student is untalented or lacking in brilliance, but because he is stubbornly determined to keep on doing what he's been doing even if that involves irrelevance. So I'll wind up on that note.

TRIFFIN: On the whole, I agree with Leonard's brilliant summary. There is one point, however, that he seems to have missed—that if we really do face the need for a slowdown of world economic growth, this is going to make far more acute the problem of equity, both within and between nations. My second point is that we may need to look at the question of the division of time between work and leisure. It is a striking fact that the working week is still just about—not quite—what it was in the 1930s, despite the enormous growth of productivity during the past four decades. One would have thought that some of the increase in productivity would have been devoted to increased leisure and cultural pursuits instead of increased production. My final remark is very brief; Professor Haberler can correct me if I'm wrong, but it seems to me that the word "depression" was used before the 1930s.

HABERLER: Oh, yes.

Chairman THORP: I might just inject here that so many people have said that we would never have another depression that we obviously can't admit that we've got one; we have to use another word for it.

SCITOVSKY: I would like to enlarge a little on what Leonard Silk and Robert Triffin have said about the equity aspect of the problem of growth. One of the most striking differences between the developed and the developing countries is in their per capita consumption of energy. I think it was Schumacher who made some very striking and very frightening estimates showing that if the developing countries are to come close to our level and type of development, their demand for energy will increase by a substantial multiple; I don't remember the exact figure, but it was something like a multiple of three or four. That, of course, creates a very difficult problem. We have been trying to help the developing countries to develop, and we are beginning to realize that for them to develop in the direction and degree in which we have developed may well be an utter impossibility. But on what moral basis can we advise them to develop in a different direction as long as we stick to our own ways?

SCHMIDT: Two points. First, Leonard, did you say D+? Was that with or without grade inflation, because whether it's on the old scale or the new scale makes a big difference. That leads me to my next point; I don't think we've done badly at all. I think the floating-rate system has made it possible for us to get through a period that was extremely difficult. Without that system, the world would be in one heck of a mess. So I don't think that the state of economics is all that bad.

SILK: That's the plus.

SCHMIDT: I thought it was the B.

SILK: No, my grade was a D—D as in dog.

SCHMIDT: Yes, but with grade inflation, that's a B.

HINSHAW: I haven't the slightest desire to get into a substantive debate with my good friend, Wilson Schmidt, but I really cannot agree with him that floating rates have been a great plus in the present situation. I think that they must be assigned much of the blame for double-digit inflation. Of course I may be somewhat biased on this subject because of the additional risks and worries, under floating rates, of planning an international monetary conference. The headaches can be rather enormous.

JAMISON: On the growth issue, I have heard various people talk about zero economic growth as a desirable aim. But in our present society with its present structure, it seems to me that zero economic growth implies, at least approximately, zero employment growth. That hardly makes sense at a time when we are having a tremendous wave of young people pouring into the labor market—the people who were born in the late 1940s and throughout the 1950s. This tidal wave of young people is substantially expanding the labor supply, which means that if we have zero employment growth we will be confronted with skyrocketing unemployment and welfare rolls. So, to me, zero economic growth is intolerable. Some accommodation has to be made. Even if we can't have as much growth in the future in the form of physical output, we can have an expansion of growth in services to absorb the mushrooming labor supply. If we don't attend to this problem, the economy is in real trouble.

SOHMEN: Well, I hope that nobody advocates zero growth in terms of high unemployment rates. But we live in a world with high external diseconomies in the form of smog, pollution, re- source depletion, and other unpleasant facts, so that we need to have a reassessment of the kinds of commodities that we want to produce—a reassessment which takes into account all these external effects. If we put the right price on them—and that is what the zero-growth people advocate—what would emerge, I think, would be a positive rate of growth of certain things which so far have been neglected.

TRIFFIN: Would leisure be one of those things?

SOHMEN: Good leisure—not leisure in smog.

JAMISON: Voluntary leisure instead of enforced leisure?

SOHMEN: Yes. Economists should be more aware than they are that there are certain things which cannot be priced very exactly but which have human value nevertheless. The better world I have in mind would be one in which we may have to use resources which are more costly in terms of traditional price systems but which at the same time generate fewer nega- tive externalities—a world of full employment and a positive rate of growth of certain amenities which until now have been neglected in traditional GNP accounting.

SALANT: Just a remark about the state of the art of eco- nomics. It seems to me that there are some rivals for the prize for the most contentious discipline, and I'm not sure that economics takes it. As to any confusion in the state of theory, I think economists are more aware of their own confusions than

they are of the confusions in other subjects. My friends in
theoretical physics have told me how upsetting it was a few
decades ago when they kept discovering more atomic particles.
The number was then up in about the thirties, I think; now it is
close to a hundred, and the theory is in a state of complete confusion. I don't know that economics is too much worse off. But
I think that a good deal of the controversy about inflation, for
example, arises from the attempt to tag some single factor as
the cause. If, instead of trying to isolate one or another thing
as the cause, we talked about the complete set of conditions
necessary for a given result—inflation in this case—much confusion and imprecision would disappear.

With regard to the recession-depression issue, I think there
ought to be a ban on discussion of these labels. That's a verbal
discussion, and I think that, in this one case, members should
walk out of the room in a body when the subject comes up, because it's not substantive. The question is not what tag to put
on something but what the something is.

WALLICH: My remarks relate to the discussion on inflation.
I think we have made some progress in that analysis. We have
enough experience with inflation in the United States and other
countries so that we can derive a certain pattern. Now the pattern is not the old type that we used to teach our students and
I, for one, am quite ready to confess to error. I had always
assumed that the main form of inflation is demand-pull—that
government or business borrows too much and that prices run
away from wages. What we see now is quite a different pattern.
We see rising wages dominating all other sources of inflation,
no matter how the inflation started. Whether the initial source
is a rise in the price of oil, food shortages, a cyclical coincidence of peaks, or other factors, we always end up with wage
inflation, and from then on the process continues in a self-
sustaining rhythm. And the pattern of this inflation is not that
prices run away from wages, but the other way about; profit
margins shrink, liquidity shrinks, and firms pay taxes on profits that are illusory. The end is illiquidity and then insolvency.

In England, we have seen this process going through several
more rounds, with the government finally having to intervene
directly to allow price increases and to permit bank credit expansion so that firms can continue in business. In the U. S.
case, we have seen what inflation does to particular industries.
Inflation has hurt very badly the utilities. It has hurt the real-
estate investment trusts, which have other problems as well.

And we see a number of firms that now are far less comfortable financially than one would have thought.

This is the pattern of inflation in the mid-1970s. It deliquifies the economy, then it tends to make the economy insolvent, so that an increasing number of enterprises need government support—barely meeting their payrolls, unable to invest, with little prospect for growth or for additional jobs. That, I think, is the predictable pattern of continued inflation, and that is why I place a very high priority on ending inflation—subject, of course, to avoiding a depression as well as to compensating the personal suffering caused by unemployment.

HABERLER: Mr. Chairman, you asked that we take a broad look at our problems from the international standpoint. Let me do that, but first let me say that, from a world standpoint, the most important thing is for the biggest country in the world, the United States, to put its house in order. If the United States were able to stop its inflation or slow it down without a steep recession, the whole world picture would look quite different. If, on the contrary, the United States goes into a deeper recession and its inflation does not go down, then the world picture is very bleak. So the first priority is that the United States should get out of its rut.

How do we do that? In the short run, I think, the prospects are not too bad. We shall spend our way out of the recession, I suppose, and it is possible—I would say even likely—that inflation will go down a little faster than the gloomy forecast in the President's budget message. But the danger is that if we are lucky and the recession is V-shaped—fast down and fast up—the inflation will also be V-shaped. This, I think is the big danger—that a year or two from now we might have 15 percent inflation instead of the 10 percent we have now.

Now here we have this dilemma of recession with inflation, or stagflation. To my mind, stagflation is simply a later stage of inflation; it is the predictable consequence of prolonged inflation, because if inflation continues as long as we have had it— more or less since the end of the war—naturally everybody expects it to go on. Everybody takes steps to anticipate the inflation, with the result that a situation is reached where, simply to slow down the inflation, not to stop it, puts us into a recession—or, one step further, where just reducing the acceleration of inflation causes trouble. This, I think, is predictable, and has been pointed out by a number of people.

How do we deal with this problem? Without the recession, of course, it was impossible to do anything about inflation, but I agree with Henry Wallich that monetary policy alone cannot solve the problem. And I agree with him that there is such a thing as a wage-push. The British example is most striking, where wages now rise, I think, by about 30 percent and consumer prices by about 20 percent; wages outrun prices. The situation isn't this bad in the United States, and the wage-push will probably be less in the near future because of unemployment. But I'm pretty sure that the labor unions will make up for lost time. This, I think, is really the longer-run basic problem, and I cannot share the optimism of my monetarist friends that if we simply stop expanding the money supply too fast, then everything will fall in line. We don't live in that kind of world anymore.

Just one more remark. It's not only the labor unions but the government itself. In hundreds of ways, the government does the same thing the unions do. The latest example is when agricultural prices went down a little bit; immediately there was a movement to boost support prices for agricultural products, with a bill to that effect submitted to Congress. When producers are unable to organize themselves into effective monopolies, the government steps in and does it for them. These things have to be changed; otherwise, I'm afraid, we shall get only a brief relaxation of stagflation trouble and will be in even greater difficulties in the future.

DE CECCO: Mr. Jamison has kindly provided us with a sheet which shows us the gross national products of all the larger countries in the world for 1973. One interesting fact that emerges is that the GNP for the United States is about equal to the total for the nine countries of the European Community. That is something rather new. It wasn't like that ten years ago and, if the present trend continues, the United States will become a less and less important part of the picture.

Now what does this mean? If one indulges one's Italian tendency to look at the past and to judge the future by what has happened before, then one might draw a parallel between the United States of today and the Britain of 1914. Some people have advanced the notion that Vietnam is the U.S. equivalent of the Boer War. I don't know about that, but there is a disturbing similarity. What I'm interested in is what this all means in terms of world monetary order. It would seem to me that the

role of the dollar is bound to diminish, because the United
States is not as powerful, relatively speaking, as it used to
be and cannot shoulder all the burdens by itself. At the same
time, we Europeans have become used to being free riders.
We are free riders in the field of defense, where we witness
the incredible situation of 200,000 American troops defending
seven of the most powerful countries in the West. This state
of affairs, I think, has never happened before, and I don't think
it will be tolerated for very long. Now this may not be a purely
economic question, but it is certainly a question of political
economy, and I think all these birds will be coming home to
roost in the next few years—especially if the growth in U.S.
GNP continues to lag behind that of Europe.

GRASSMAN: The various speakers this morning have
touched only in passing on the international monetary aspects
of the problems we face at the present time. I would like to
raise a few international monetary matters that have not yet
received attention around this table.

One key issue, of course, is the international role of the
dollar in the immediate future. I think that it's important to
realize that it is the reserve role of the dollar that lies at the
heart of the working or, if you will, the nonworking of the system. I would say that the reserve role is the only significant
role that the dollar plays on the international market. To understand this, let us just briefly look at what the dollar means
for business firms, commercial banks, and central banks in
the three familiar functions of money—namely, as a medium
of exchange, as a unit of account, and as a store of value.

The medium-of-exchange function in international transactions is performed by local currencies in the convertible system that we have today. Firms have no need to hold foreign-
denominated assets in order to settle international transactions.
As to the unit-of-account function, we know that, both for commercial banks and for central banks, the dollar performs an
interesting role. But this really doesn't create a demand for,
or supply of, dollars.

The central role of the dollar as an international money
lies in the store-of-value function—in other words, in the
dollar's use as a reserve currency. It was the reserve role
of the dollar which enabled the United States to have a passive
balance-of-payments policy. Contrary to Professor Mundell,
this was not a forced passivity arising from the unit-of-account

function of the dollar.   It was the reserve role which alone
made possible a passive policy—a policy which for a time,
of course, was profitable.   But there was no forced passivity
in the system.

VIII. SUMMARY AND CRITIQUE

Lord Robbins

Chairman THORP: Earlier today, we heard a number of views on the present state of economics. Not long ago, I compared the economics and physics textbooks which I had used as an undergraduate at Amherst College with those used now. Although both had changed greatly, the economics textbook had changed much more than the physics text. One of the reasons is that physicists have what one might call unchanging subject matter; they simply find out new things about it. We economists have continually changing subject matter, and this greatly complicates any effort to arrive at ultimate truth. Economics is a developing subject that tries to be relevant to the problems that we have today. How successful we at this conference have or have not been in this endeavor I will leave for Lord Robbins to judge as he summarizes our discussion.

Lord ROBBINS: Everything which you have just said, Willard, makes my task more difficult. The conference has been an extremely good conference; I think we should all agree about that. But it has covered an immense range of material, not all of a homogeneous nature. I got up at 5 o'clock this morning to try to put my notes in some sort of order, and you will realize as my observations proceed that my success has not been great. I remember that in the Book of Genesis it is said that on the Sabbath Day the Lord ceased from His work and found that it was good. Well, on this seventh day, I have not ceased from my work, and I find that it's bad!

129

But let me get down to the humble job that has been assigned
to me of acting as Moderator of this conference. What I propose to do is to try to bring out the salient features of the various discussions that we have had. I am treating them in reverse
order—that is to say, starting with oil, which we discussed last,
then going on to inflation and depression, which I am treating
a little less briefly, and winding up with a rather more extensive
treatment of the problems of exchange rates and international
monetary systems.

I shall eschew the temptation to comment upon the more dis-
cursive observations that have been made this morning, though
I will give myself the luxury of one remark—that I am extremely
surprised to find that a learned society of this sort, in the discussion of pro-growth or anti-growth, made no reference to the
population problem. Now whatever the classical economists
left out, Leonard Silk, they did not leave that subject out, and
there is really quite a lot buried in the dark backward abysm
of time, obscured from us now by the necessity of reading so
much contemporary literature, which deals with the problem
of scarcity in your sense. I commend Jevons on the coal question, for instance. However, I shall focus in my summary on
issues rather than on individual contributions, although I shall
continually be referring to individual contributions as a reminder
of the salient points that have been made. And may I please apologize in advance if I don't do justice either to those whom I cite
or to those whom I omit to cite. This is due to incompetence on
my part and to the difficulties of compression.

I

Let me now begin with the discussion which is most recently
in our minds—the discussion we had yesterday afternoon about
the economic impact of the changes which have taken place in
the markets for oil and energy. I don't think that there is any
need for me to fill in very much the background of this problem.
We had a masterly survey of it all by Isaiah Frank which will be
fresh in the minds of all of you. But I don't recollect that we
had much discussion of what to me is the most important aspect
of the whole thing—namely, its political complexion: the diplomatic pressures which may be unfortunately looming ahead if
talks in the Middle East break down. Well, certainly these things
were in the back of our minds, and there was some recognition
of the economic cost of providing adequate security against

contingencies of a military nature. The costs were drawn to
our attention by Wilson Schmidt, and Henry Wallich in his extremely helpful survey brought the security aspect into the
limelight.

But the main discussion focused on the burden of the rise in
the price of oil. I think on that point there was a good deal more
consensus than on many of the points we discussed. Under the
guidance of Henry Wallich, most of us, I think, came to the conclusion that any sharp contrast between the monetarist and the
Keynesian approach to matters of this sort was uncalled for; the
two modes of approach simply brought to light different aspects
of what is fundamentally one and the same problem. On the
whole, if I'm not mistaken, the sense of the meeting was that,
statistically considered, the burden of the higher oil price—at
least so far as the industrial powers are concerned—has not
been insupportable.

Leonard Silk reminded us that we mustn't concentrate simply
on the burden of the rise in the price of oil; we must also pay
some attention to the rise in the price of substitute sources of
energy. And Mrs. Whitman made some salutary remarks on
the importance of the structure of the various economies affected
by the very sharp change in relative prices. My own judgment
on this matter is that we ought to go much further than generalizations of this sort. We will do well to keep in mind the different
conditions in our different industrial countries as regards the
rapidity of their response to the impact of changes of this nature.
But I'm sure we should all agree that, while the changes which
have taken place are little short of a catastrophe to some of the
developing countries, they constitute an awkwardness rather
than a catastrophe for most of the industrial communities.

We had a good deal of talk—a survey, so to speak—of the
working of the mechanism of transfer. Arthur Young and others
made reassuring remarks about the strength of potential demand
from at least some of the OPEC countries, a matter which I
touched on a little in my opening observations. I think one can
greatly underestimate the potential demand from countries such
as Iran, Iraq, Algeria, and perhaps one or two others. We've
been reminded, too, by Robert Triffin and others of the possibility of easing the process of transfer by stretching it out through
time, either by way of long-term contracts or by way of inducing
the recipients of the transfer to use their funds to make long-
term investments. Frank Tamagna held out the tempting aspect
that if this response were to take place, we should be in the

position, so to speak, of having some hostages for future good
behavior. Others drew our attention to the importance of not
being too much alarmed about the inability of the existing banking system to deal with the problem of recycling. We were
reminded that a good deal of recycling is already taking place
and that the impact has been, on the whole, very much less
than might have been at first supposed.

I personally agree that the transfer problem can be overestimated. I think transfer problems have been overestimated
to a large extent in history. Reference was made to the transfer problem created, or alleged to be created, by the Versailles
settlement, and no doubt there was a good deal of political upset
and consequential economic dislocation arising from that source.
But in my judgment—and here I would part company almost completely with Maynard Keynes—the trouble was not so much the
difficulty of reasonable transfer (Keynes was quite right, of
course, in insisting on the absurdity of astronomical transfer)
but rather was due to the mess made by the politicians.

And then our conversation wandered to the statistical assumptions which it is desirable to make in trying to get our ideas into
shape in regard to the magnitude of the burden caused by the
higher oil price. Professor Douglass drew attention to the possibility of some reduction in the present price of oil, and one of
our members, Robert Aliber, made the same point last week in
an article in the Wall Street Journal. Personally, I find there
is a good deal in that. I can't resist the impression that, politics and political catastrophe apart, the OPEC powers have
rather overplayed their hand.

Finally, we were led in this way to some discussion of recently ventilated proposals concerning the possibility of agreements regarding floor prices—proposals which, although not
confirmed at a high official level, were not altogether denied.
And I suppose this must have rung a bell with some members
about the probable reaction to such proposals of the Scottish
nationalists, who certainly would be very mortified indeed to
think that the gigantic installations which are presently being
erected at enormous cost might be rendered unprofitable by
too great a movement back toward the price of oil prevailing
before the formation of the cartel. Here I detected a general
agreement that, whatever is necessary by way of reassurance
for national-security reasons, floor prices are not the best way
to deal with the problem. I personally see very great dangers
in giving wide currency to the idea of floor prices. Once that

becomes a respectable idea, hordes of people will want to apply
the same concept to other commodities.

I must say that my own personal experience during the war,
when I negotiated with the State Department and other important
organs of the United States government, and with representa-
tives of the commodity-producing world as a whole, leads me
to extreme pessimism in this respect. We submitted extremely
enlightened and sophisticated ideas, devised by Maynard Keynes,
with regard to evening out small fluctuations about the secular
trend in commodity prices. These were rejected with contumely
by the producers and by the American Department of Agriculture.
Rigid quantitative restrictions were the least they would agree
to. And they certainly represented the opinion that discussion
should not start on the assumption that current prices were at
all satisfactory from their point of view.

II

Well, so much for the OPEC and all those evils. Now let me
come to what, in the broad universe of discourse, is something
much more interesting and much more important: the problem
of inflation and depression. I don't recollect that we had much
talk about rates of inflation; they are too painfully obvious all
around us for one to wish to dwell on them. How tedious it is
when one notices that the price has gone up from yesterday to
today—which not infrequently happens at the London School of
Economics refectory. But we did have a very serious and weighty
reminder from Bob Solomon on the extent to which the depression
or recession has already progressed. And although I'm sure we
should all agree with the assurances which are given in various
quarters that what the United States is going through is not to be
compared with what happened during the 1930s, the recession is
considerably more serious than anything that has happened for
quite a long time.

Having worked out a general perspective of inflation and depression, we then proceeded to minuter considerations. I don't
think we paid much attention in the course of our discussions to
the problem raised by Henry Wallich this morning of the definition of inflation. If I may speak personally, I should be completely in agreement with the diagnosis which he gave of the
course of inflation in various leading countries at the present
time. I should not be prepared, I think, to stand quite so much
in a white sheet as he did as regards the teaching of the young

in the past; I don't really think we can assume that demand inflation has disappeared from the world. I can certainly think of
some Latin American countries where we could find examples
of that sort of thing. And when I think of the position of my own
unfortunate country, which is certainly very much beset at the
present moment by cost-push inflation, I am quite sure that
there have been demand-pull elements in that history since the
war. I speak not simply in an impressionistic way, but have
very much in mind the earlier period before the inflation became
so serious. There is an excellent book by Dow which I think
holds the scales evenly, and shows that evil can arise from one
side or the other. But I thoroughly agree with what was said
about the importance of cost inflation by Henry Wallich and by
Gottfried Haberler.

We concentrated during the main debate on the causes of inflation. And here, I suppose, the center of gravity of the discussion was Robert Triffin's valuable presentation of the growth
of monetary reserves and his classification of the categories
into which the various parts of that growth were to be placed.
I don't think anybody called into question Professor Triffin's
statistics, but there were questions raised as regards the direct
connection between the growth of reserves and the development
of the money supply—whether M-1 or any other of the Ms. Marcus Fleming and Walter Salant called attention to the fact that
there was no exact correlation—which, indeed, Robert was perfectly willing to admit. I think we should all agree that the connection between reserves and the flows of money is a highly
complicated one in detail.

I couldn't help thinking, as I was sitting here writing notes,
that there was one case, at any rate, where there was a reverse
connection capable of an immensely simple explanation. It seems
to be thought by some people that it is paradoxical that some
countries which had achieved the highest reserves had a low rate
of monetary expansion. The case of Germany leaps to mind.
Well, members of the conference, I should simply say that this
was a case of the reward of virtue. Or, if you want to put the
matter another way, the twice-burnt child dreads the fire. The
imprudent inflation of other countries caused the Germans to
become more competitive than otherwise might have been the
case and, rather than import other people's inflation just in
order to help the other people out, they have pursued a reasonably prudent policy—punctuated occasionally by hesitation in
that respect—and consequently have had a much lower rate of

inflation than most of the rest of us.

After some discussion of the causes of inflation, we directed our attention to the central problem of the continuation of inflation despite recession.   I think Bob Solomon endorsed that part of my diagnosis in my opening observations regarding the importance of paying attention to time lags in this connection.   He also endorsed the diagnosis which Gottfried Haberler and others made about the predominance of the cost-push influences now. I personally, only a week out from Great Britain, regard what is going on there as an absolute model of the pattern of that kind of inflation.   Whatever the origins of British inflation, whether on the demand side or on the supply side, there is no doubt at all about the cost influences at the present time.   The rate of increase of prices last year was just a little short of 20 percent; the rate of increase of earnings, despite a very small increase of productivity, was over 29 percent.

Perhaps the cost-push influences are slowing down in some countries, but I am inclined to think that the commitment to policies of maintaining high levels of employment irrespective of the price of labor have tended to inhibit the curbs that might otherwise have been applied.   And I do ask myself, speaking personally, whether we economists in the last quarter of this century haven't perhaps rather limited ourselves by focusing too much on high levels of employment as the sole objective of policy, to the rejection of the more old-fashioned idea of the objective of policy being the maintenance of the value of money, coupled with the new knowledge that, if there were increases in the value of money giving rise to severe unemployment, it was legitimate to do all sorts of things with the monetary system which our fathers would have thought to be unorthodox and ill-advised.

We all agreed that the situation we confront now is a novel situation—one which, as Gottfried Haberler pointed out, poses a nasty dilemma: we want to stop inflation, and we do not want to cause unemployment and unused capacity. Here we had a very interesting and important discussion which was triggered off by Arthur Laffer's stimulating contribution, reinforced by a sensational telegram from an absent friend, dear Bob Mundell, exhorting a tight monetary policy and an enormous cut in U.S. taxes.   Before I review the disquiet which was felt in certain quarters about this, let me say that I gather that Laffer and Mundell, with whom I feel much instinctive sympathy, are certainly not opposed to restraints on inflation by operations on

the money side. On the contrary, these valiant exponents are
the soul of prudence in this respect. The novelty of their approach, whether right or wrong, is that they seek to focus more
attention than most of the rest of us on the possibility of stimulating output. So, operating on the goods side of the Fisher
equation, Professor Laffer in his remarks here dwelt in particular on the disincentive effects of transfer payments and
various inimical forms of taxation.

Well, needless to say, this gave rise to a great deal of some
of the most entertaining discussion. There was some skepti-
cism expressed concerning the pure theory of the disincentive
effect of transfer payments. I'm not quite sure what the consensus was there. I know what I think myself: that there is a
wide band of uncertainty concerning the effects of such transfers
on the will to work—whether they make you work a bit more or
work a bit less. But I'm equally certain concerning the disincentive effects of very high marginal tax rates. Who but a fool
would refuse to admit that there would be some disincentive
effect if the marginal tax rate were 100 percent? Well, I ask,
what is the big difference between 100 percent and 98 percent—
the marginal rate of taxation in Great Britain on investment
income? I can't help thinking that there must come a point at
which even the most zealous entrepreneurs and other inhabitants
of the world of industry get a little discouraged.

But at this point Gottfried commented that the Mundell-Laffer
proposals could take effect only in the long run, whereas the
problem with which we were confronted was a short-term or
medium-term problem. I don't think that Gottfried disassociated
himself from all talk of the disincentive effect of taxation; I have
a feeling that he would certainly be on what I should regard as
the right side there if he were directly under cross-examination.
But he did actually use the word "gimmick" as regards the short
period. And vigorous responses were made to that sort of accu-
sation by Laffer, who drew attention to various forms of taxation
other than social-security contributions which he felt had an
inimical effect on enterprise in the fairly short period.

I myself felt at that juncture that, whatever may be the doubt
about the disincentive effects of transfer payments on the goods
side, I have absolutely no doubt at all about the restraining effect
on economic growth of restrictive practices—at any rate, in my
own country. A few months ago, when we had a three-day working week because of an industrial dispute in the coal mines, GNP
flickered downward by an eyelash, so to speak. People wanted

to take home, roughly speaking, the same pay package insofar as that was possible. Now far be it for me to suggest that this sort of effort would be possible over the long run. But speaking with a certain amount of personal contact with industry in one or two quarters, I would say—and I'm aware that I'm sticking my neck out—that if the restrictive practices in the main industrial sectors in Great Britain were removed, it would be possible to contemplate an almost discontinuous rise in the level of production of up to 20 percent over a comparatively short period.

And this reminds me of Egon Sohmen's very interesting remarks about Germany and the comparison with Great Britain. I'm not quite so clear as he was about the connection between the frame of mind of management and the frame of mind of labor unions in the United Kingdom, any more than I was clear about Marcus Fleming's remark about the prevalence of gentlemen in the upper ranks of British industry at the present time. What Marcus said might have been true twenty-five years ago, but I think the technicians and hard-working people have won their way through now. But I do agree 100 percent with Professor Sohmen's statement that if there were less monopoly on the trade-union side and more competition, not only in Great Britain but in the world generally, cost inflation would be much less of a problem.

Well, what do we do about this nasty dilemma? Some members of the conference—Messrs. Jamison and McClellan, for instance—still are disposed to regard inflation as the main enemy. I personally would regard inflation—cost inflation—rather than depression as the main enemy in Great Britain. Other members of the conference, chiefly citizens of this great Union, naturally concerned with the recession in the United States, were inclined to regard the degree to which the recession had advanced as being the main problem. I don't think of any consensus here, but there was a highly interesting discussion in the course of which Messrs. Bob Solomon and Walter Salant made what to me were extremely stimulating remarks about the part which the projection of full-employment budgets might play in suggesting possible cures for recession. I found all that very thought-provoking and pregnant with possibilities as regards practical action. But I've been inclined to feel—and I've said this privately to Walter and Bob—that they need to introduce an additional variable into their budgeting nowadays. The idea of full-employment budgeting was developed at a time when the

value of money, although not constant, was not worrying people
very much. But I think that when we talk about full-employment
budgeting now, we've got to state quite explicitly what assumptions we are making about the rate of increase of wages. And
if that's germane in the United States, how much more germane
it is on the other side of the Atlantic.

Which brings me back to the opposition of employment policy
and price stabilization. Can we pursue without reservation a
full-employment policy if the rate of wages is exogenously imposed? Ought not the guarantee nowadays to be, not full employment whatever it costs at whatever price of labor, but rather
to be high levels of employment at prices which, if not constant,
are only rising at a tolerable rate? And we need not assume
that the trade unions consist of complete automatons who have
no opportunity of making up their minds for themselves. We
know that they do make up their minds in all sorts of ways.
Ought we not leave them a choice?

III

I come now to the nonstop Friday discussion about exchanges
and the monetary system, which, in a way, had a wider horizon
and wider implications for speculative thought than anything that
happened yesterday. Our discussion took its rise from doubts
or approbations regarding floating exchange rates. Some members of the conference had been leaning toward fixity, others to
clean floating, and perhaps I may say that there seemed to be
less of a head-on clash on this matter this time than there was
the last time we discussed the subject. Perhaps those of us,
including myself, who have some leanings toward fixity have
deferred a bit to the temporary state of the world, while others—
no one here, of course—who thought that all problems were to
be solved by free floating have come to the conclusion that there
may be some slight disadvantages. But I think we were all agreed
that in the present state of the world, with different national policies going in different directions (not to mention the antics of
the oil cartel), floating rates are here for some time.

And having in various ways given recognition to this proposition, the conference then began to address itself to a very interesting question: whether floating itself is an inflationary influ-
emce, a question which was raised with great succinctness and
force by Randall Hinshaw and by Tibor Scitovsky. Well, here
I would repeat an intervention which I had permission to make

at that stage: I do think that it's very important that we should
rid this question of ambiguity.

First of all, does the fact of floating breed irresponsibility
on the part of governments and others? Now I can testify to
you that there is at least one government in the world whose
late Chancellor of the Exchequer confessed, not, of course, to
irresponsibility, but to a feeling of a greater sense of elbowroom now that at last the pound was free—oh, I've let out his
nationality, but let that pass. And I really must tell you that
my observation has roped in a few cases in which some degree
of irresponsibility of that sort has been fostered in the breasts
of those extremely nice and well-intentioned people who are
leaders of the trade unions. Under the old Bretton Woods international monetary system of fixed exchange rates, I think your
more sensible trade-union leaders, when deciding how much of
the cake to ask for next time, did have half an eye, at any rate,
on the possibilities of gold flows and financial crisis, whereas
once the pound was freed, well, the free rate takes care of all
that—that's the slogan.

The second question, which is the one I fancy Randall and
Tibor had in mind and which is intellectually much more interesting, is whether floating is inflationary in itself. Does the
fact that there is a downward movement of the exchange rate
breed inflation, other things being equal? Well, I'm not sure
that we reached a conclusion about that. I seem to remember
that there is a very good chapter in James Meade's voluminous
treatment of international problems in which he demonstrates
that for his ideal system of clean floating—and James is the
platonic archetype of the clean floater—there ought to be a slight
tightening up of interest rates and monetary controls when there
is a downward movement in the rate of exchange, just to make
sure that a sort of cumulative Wicksellian process would not be
inaugurated. Perhaps that is the sort of thing which Tibor and
Randall had in mind.

But then there is a third question—a frightfully important
practical question: does floating breed internal repercussions
of a secondary order? Are wages linked to the cost of living?
And if the rate floats downward and the cost of living goes up,
will there be an additional encouragement to wage inflation?
I don't say that this possibility is inevitable, but it is certainly
not remote. I sometimes think of what might happen in Great
Britain in a financial crisis—which is not absolutely excluded—

if the lenders were to cease lending the billions of pounds which they are lending at present and were to take their money elsewhere. I'm not saying that such a crisis is probable; I'm simply saying that if it happened and if the pound were to drop from $2.40, where it is now, to say $1.50, there certainly would be repercussions on the level of money wages quite irrespective of the movement of real productivity.

Well, leaving all that on one side, we had some discussion—very technically expert in some respects—about some of the disadvantages of floating, even managed floating. Although I don't think she attached great importance to the point, Mrs. Whitman called attention to the absence of adequate forward markets. Some members, such as Mr. Grassman, felt that this hadn't had a very bad effect on world trade thus far, but I did notice some disquiet. Marcus Fleming, who confessed himself to having been an outright floater at one stage, told us that he had moved a bit toward the center. Having known Marcus for at least the last forty years, I regard a pronouncement of that sort as carrying a great deal of weight. And others expressed aspirations for some mutual recognition of the need for coordination and rules.

This discussion of rules and regulations involved us in some of the most difficult questions of policy. I think we all agreed that there was a considerable messiness about present arrangements. Most members, if they advocated some management, as Gottfried does, deprecated the expression "dirty floating," and thrust it from them, so to speak. Some members were not apparently disturbed by the messiness. Professor Aliber's utopia, or provisional utopia, was a state of affairs in which every national area had achieved stability in its own internal arrangements, with international order emerging as a sort of unexpected—or expected—bonus. But, dealing with the real world, one knows that it's not a bit like that and that the areas of solidification are not necessarily even the areas of sovereign states. The dollar is not only supreme in the United States, but arrangements with the dollar, linkages with the dollar, prevail elsewhere. Up to a little time ago, there was a very considerable link between sterling and other areas.

IV

So this leads us to what to me is one of the most fascinating questions of all—the question of the optimal area of monetary

independence. Now I have studied this a little, and I gather
that a very powerful book is shortly to be issued by Tom Willett, from which I hope to learn more. My impression is that
the theory—which goes back to Myrdal, doesn't it? —hinges on
the measurement of the degree of mobility of factors of production, and where you have a frightful stickiness of factor mobility, there, perhaps, you can draw a circle and say that changes
in real income will be brought about by changes in the exchange
rate, but that, within those areas, they will be brought about by
changes in the monetary mechanism. In my opening remarks,
I ventured to say that this did place a good deal of weight on the
persistence of money illusion, and, in spite of a little reproach
on the quiet from Tom Willett, I still believe that there's a good
deal in that.

Of course, I wouldn't argue that the total effects, the distri-
butional effects, of a change in the rate of exchange are exactly
the same effects as a corresponding change in costs brought
about by money flows induced by the old specie-flow mechanism
of metallic standards. But I certainly find the idea of optimal
areas extremely interesting to speculate about, though not at all
easy to reconcile with the facts of the messy world as it confronts us at the moment. If the unfortunately separate states
of Western Europe, after a due period of experimentation and
adjustment, were really to achieve a common money, I can conceive of a sort of float between that monetary unit and the dollar
which could be contained within reasonable limits and conducted
with reasonable decency by matey conversations between U.S.
officials and whoever represented the Community.

But leaving all that apart, I would like to plug my personal
reminder that monetary separatism persists only because of
politically imposed restrictions. The whole world hungers and
thirsts—although it doesn't work very hard to satisfy the hunger
and thirst—for a common money. We talk about the centrifugal
impulses created by independent centers of money supply, but,
though expert audiences like this know all about it, we keep mum
about the centripetal tendencies—the desperate desire of people
to get around the restrictions on holding foreign currencies and
on making contracts in the money which is expected to fluctuate
least. I myself believe that if all these restrictions were removed, then we would speedily see emerging some sort of common money which would make all the national currencies obsolete
within a comparatively short period of time. We saw the thing
actually happening in practice with the emergence of gold in the

nineteenth century and the falling away of silver. We saw the
thing in practice in Germany and central Europe in the hyper-
inflations when people took to making all their contracts in
dollars or in sterling. And it would happen today if it were
not for political tendencies.

Well, I don't suggest that this is anything more than a sort
of incidental observation. I don't believe that governments are
going to do this sort of thing, and so we are still confronted
with our problem. But this does bring me to the noble and
splendid pronouncement of my old friend, John Parke Young—
his fine enunciation of an ideal, his exhortations to proceed
with the creation of a world money which would enable the economic activities of the world to go on with a minimum of fuss
and friction. His proposal, as I understand it, is some trans-
mogrification of SDRs to provide this basis. I detect a certain
kinship between his exhortations and the original draft of the
Keynes Plan, with the "bancor" and so on, but with more cau-
tions inserted as regards the inflationary tendencies of the
bancor.

I think we ought to take this very seriously even if we don't
think that it's frightfully practical. It clears the mind very much
to think of noble aspirations of this sort—aspirations which most
of us would willingly achieve if we thought we had the means to
do so. And I would agree that it is worth thinking about the SDRs
in this connection. Like St. Paul, the SDRs were, in a way, born
out of due season; they were invented to supply a lack of liquidity
in a world which suddenly became more liquid than it ever had
been in human history. And that's an ironic circumstance, though
it need not detain us very long. I still think that, in spite of the
oddness of conception and parturition, so to speak, the inten-
tions were very honorable, and I also think that the SDRs may
contain a speck of the ideal.

Well, now, where are we? Professor Oliver suggested that
I, as one of the surviving members of the Bretton Woods conference, should outline a plan. Far be it from me. But various
suggestions have been made which I think deserve just a little
attention before I close.

Robert Triffin ventilated the idea of a unit of account which
would be useful in commercial and financial transactions—a
basket of SDRs which he thought would provide a more stable
unit of account than those presently available. I find the idea
immensely stimulating, but, as I said to Robert as we walked
away, I find some difficulty in regarding this as ideal over time.

Suppose the basket not only became a unit of account but also
was developing into some sort of common medium of exchange,
and compare the purchasing power of the contents of the basket,
say, in 1948 with its purchasing power in terms of commodities
in the mid-1970s — it certainly wouldn't be ideal. But I'm looking forward very much indeed to reading Robert's paper on this
subject, because I think that it may very easily guide us into
fruitful prospects. What we clearly need to satisfy John Parke
Young's exhortation is something which not only is a unit of
account but also is quite overtly a medium of exchange, so con-
trolled as to maintain relative monetary stability.

I do think that we are still a long way from all this, and I feel
that we are longer away than I sometimes hope when I listen to
some of you high U. S. experts, with whom I should simply love
to be in agreement all the time. I feel a little bit of a cad to
find myself in disagreement with Walter Salant or Bob Solomon,
for instance; I know that they want to phase gold out completely
and have nothing but paper standards managed according to the
most enlightened principles.

But don't think that I am going to end with a plea for a return
to gold a la Rueff or to the gold standard according to the models of Humean classical economists. I am not as unsophisti-
cated as that. Indeed, I would claim to you that I know all the
arguments against gold and could repeat them in my sleep.
But I confess that I have often wondered whether one can write
off gold completely when two-thirds of the human race do not
entirely share the views of American experts and are able to
advance the empirical fact that, with all their fluctuations,
metals have done better than paper in the past. You can't get
away from that one.

I have wondered whether gold hasn't still some role to play
as a facade in an enlightened SDR system. But not gold bars
with a fixed content. In this connection, always wishing to keep
abreast of U. S. enlightenment—so obviously the center of gravity
of enlightenment in the modern age — I reinforce myself by recol-
lecting Irving Fisher. How many of you read Irving Fisher nowadays? Jack Viner once said to me that if Irving Fisher and
Frank Taussig were rolled into one, with the intellectual acumen
of the former and the practical judgment of the latter, then America would need no economists for a hundred years. Be that as it
may, I do commend to you all the idea of Fisher's Compensated
Dollar, the weight of which, you will recall, would vary according to the most enlightened conceivable index-number device.

There you might have your facade.   None of you would be
afraid of frightful adverse consequences in the United States.
The lesser breeds without the law would be reassured about
the SDR, and the linkage with the enlightened price index number would be a greater guarantee of stability than seems likely
to be the world's fate or, at any rate, my fate in my lifetime —
although I do hope that the rest of you will have a better time
of it later on.

NAME INDEX

Aliber, Robert Z., 29-30, 47, 61-62, 68, 74, 83, 92, 104, 106, 112, 132, 140

Arndt, Sven W., 34, 82

Boulding, Kenneth E., 119

Churchill, Sir Winston, 28

De Cecco, Marcello, 49, 61, 73-74, 93, 107, 113, 114, 125-26

Douglass, Gordon K., 85, 101, 132

Exter, John, 7

Fisher, Irving, 11, 143

Fleming, J. Marcus, 30-31, 55-57, 65-66, 67, 74-75, 79-80, 81, 95, 107, 109, 134, 137, 140

Frank, Isaiah, 6, 32-33, 70, 97-101, 102, 103, 105-6, 109, 112, 114, 116, 130

Friedman, Milton, 11

Galbraith, J. K., 118

Grassman, Sven, 51-52, 103, 126-27, 140

Haberler, Gottfried, 2, 3, 15, 16, 26-27, 39, 42, 57-59, 61-62, 75, 113, 120, 121, 124-25, 134, 135, 136, 140

Hamilton, Earl J., 111

Harrod, Sir Roy, 41

Hinshaw, Randall, 1-6, 9, 41-42, 43, 46, 55, 59, 82, 121, 138, 139

Jamison, Conrad C., 47, 78, 88, 93-94, 108, 122, 125, 137

Jevons, W. S., 11, 130

Keynes, Lord, 2-3, 43, 132, 133, 142

Kindleberger, Charles P., 59

Kissinger, Henry A., 112

Kohlhagen, Steven W., 3, 48-49, 52, 82, 88

Laffer, Arthur B., 6, 30, 31, 42-43, 53-54, 71-73, 74, 75, 76, 77, 80, 82-83, 94, 111, 135, 136

Machlup, Fritz, 32, 67, 104

McClellan, H. C., 33-34, 77, 78, 137

McKinnon, Ronald I., 31, 49, 64-65, 74, 75, 76, 77

McNamara, Robert S., 32

Meade, J. E., 139

Mundell, Robert A., 4, 82, 83, 126, 135, 136

Myrdal, Gunnar, 141

Oliver, Robert W., 31-32, 42, 142

Plato, 16

Powell, Enoch, 11

Robbins, Lord, 1, 2, 6, 7-21, 23, 24, 25, 27, 30, 31, 33, 34, 37, 51, 61, 70, 78, 86, 87, 100, 114, 129-44

Roosevelt, Franklin D., 41

Rueff, Jacques, 7

SUBJECT INDEX

DATE DUE

Q 10 82	